Costa Rica Five Years after CAFTA-DR

DIRECTIONS IN DEVELOPMENT
Trade

Costa Rica Five Years after CAFTA-DR

Assessing Early Results

Friederike (Fritzi) Koehler-Geib and Susana M. Sanchez,
Editors

WORLD BANK GROUP

Contents

Tables

Foreword

This volume was motivated by a request from the Ministry of Foreign Trade (*Ministerio de Comercio Exterior* [COMEX]) of Costa Rica to evaluate the impact of the Dominican Republic–Central America–United States Free Trade Agreement (CAFTA-DR), five years after ratification. They were keen to hear from an independent, credible source about the early effects of this important treaty on the Costa Rican economy.

For us at the World Bank, this was a welcome request, considering that one of our technical teams has been deeply involved in the CAFTA-DR debates since 2002. In that year, the five Central American countries and the United States first engaged in pre-negotiation talks. I was fortunate to coordinate that team, supporting Central American governments and other stakeholders in evaluating key aspects of the treaty. We met with a large group of people engaged in discussions on agricultural and industrial good tariffs, sanitary restrictions, intellectual property rights, foreign investment, trade in services, and more, trying to assess what an agreement could mean for the economies of Central America. For those of us involved in these discussions, it proved to be very rewarding due to the breadth and richness of the exchange.

On balance, the World Bank team concluded that a free trade agreement with the United States, the largest trading partner for the five nations, would be a useful tool to promote investment, growth, and employment. However, the team highlighted that, in order to obtain the strongest positive developmental impact, Central Americans would need to resolve key bottlenecks of the development agenda—such as building critical infrastructure, removing excessive regulations, and improving education quality. Otherwise, there was a risk that the impact of the treaty could be muted. We also thought that the energetic debates around CAFTA-DR could provide an unparalleled opportunity for Central Americans to advance the development agenda in a way that would be beneficial for growth and equity, regardless of whether the agreement materialized. The World Bank's work was crystallized in 2004 with the publication of *Challenges of CAFTA-DR: Maximizing Benefits for Central America*, a book I had the pleasure to co-author with Daniel Lederman.

The topic was contentious and produced passionate exchanges in most of the countries involved. Many of the debates were serious, well informed, and allowed for the airing of important concerns. Would this really facilitate more exports from Central America? Or would it unleash a tsunami of imports that would quash local companies? Would local farmers be badly affected, particularly semi-subsistence producers of basic staples? Would there be a strong impact on foreign direct investment (FDI), as was found in Mexico during the early years of the North American Free Trade Agreement (NAFTA)? How could Central Americans ensure that the treaty would attract investment, particularly in higher value added items that could provide good quality formal jobs? For Costa Rica, many of the questions focused on the impact of the opening of the insurance and tele-communications sectors to competition. World Bank teams focused some of their work on trying to answer some of these important questions.

The chapters in this volume include the response of the World Bank to the request from Costa Rica to provide an early look at impacts of CAFTA-DR, focusing on trade and FDI flows between Costa Rica and the United States, and events in the telecom, insurance, and pharmaceutical sectors. Of course, these cannot provide a comprehensive, definitive assessment. Too little time has gone by, and the evidence is still only partial. In addition, at this early stage, it is not easy to disentangle the precise impacts of the treaty from those arising from other significant developments—such as the strong impact on growth, exports, investment, and employment during the global recession of 2009–10.

Despite these caveats and the short time since ratification, the evidence reviewed suggests that Costa Rica has derived significant positive benefits from CAFTA-DR. Export flows to the United States have risen, and prelimi-nary econometric tests suggest that the treaty has provided an extra boost. Although it is harder to measure the precise impact on FDI, it is clear that investors have continued to prefer Costa Rica over other destinations, particu-larly in the sophisticated manufacturing and service areas that the country has developed in recent years. A survey of investors performed specifically for this assessment indicates that many had CAFTA-DR on their mind when they planned their investment.

The telecommunications market has shown extraordinary growth in access and reductions in prices after the opening created by CAFTA-DR. Service supply is now abundant, prices for Internet access have been reduced dramatically, and Costa Ricans can buy a cell line with no waiting time. In the insurance sector, the opening fostered by CAFTA-DR has prompted a market in which 12 insurers compete, benefiting consumers through improved efficiency, solid growth, and product innovation. And on pharmaceuticals, preliminary evidence indicates that CAFTA-DR regulations have not noticeably restricted generic competition, drug prices, or the finances of the Costa Rican Social Security Administration (*Caja Costarricense de Seguro Social* [CCSS]).

Given the positive results obtained, a key question is: Why has this success materialized quickly for Costa Rica? Clearly, the country was in a privileged position among member countries. Decades of investment in human capital, political stability, policies supporting trade and open investment, along with citi-zen security, were responsible for a significant transformation of the economy since the 1980s. CAFTA-DR came at a good time, nearly a decade and a half after the country opted for a strategy of "smart" integration in the global economy. The "smart" part comes from its heavy emphasis in shaping the type of investment it wanted to attract—looking for investors who can bring high value added manufacturing or service.

It is indeed impressive to look at the revolutionary transformation of the Costa Rican economy after 25 years. In the mid-1980s, exports were still dominated by agricultural goods, such as coffee, bananas, and pineapples. In more recent years, exports have become increasingly diversified, with significant shares in areas such as microprocessors, medical devices, and services for back office functions. This is perhaps the most dramatic transformation of the export structure of any Latin American economy since the 1980s. CAFTA-DR seems to be contributing to deepening this important trend.

Going forward, an important research agenda remains on the impacts of CAFTA-DR. The work presented here does not include a detailed analysis of the impacts on employment, poverty, or inequality. Another important aspect that may deserve further analysis is the impact of free trade agreements on fiscal receipts and the changing structure of Costa Rican taxation associated with its strong pro-trade and pro-FDI strategy. Another aspect that should be explored is the impact on trade and investment flows within Central America, as CAFTA-DR was instrumental in deepening integration rules in the region. Finally, future work will also need to compare and contrast the impact across the other Central American member countries, as well as the Dominican Republic.

Carlos Felipe Jaramillo
Former Country Director
Central America Department

Costa Rica Five Years after CAFTA-DR • http://dx.doi.org/10.1596/978-1-4648-0568-4

Acknowledgments

This report was prepared by a team led by Friederike (Fritzi) Koehler-Geib and Susana M. Sanchez under the overall supervision and guidance of Oscar Calvo-Gonzalez (Program Leader, LCC2C), Auguste T. Kouame (Practice Manager, GMFDR), J. Humberto López (Country Director, LCC2C), and C. Felipe Jaramillo (former Country Director, LCC2C). The core team included Cinar Baymul, Mateo Clavijo, Jorge Cornick, Alejandra Castro, Diana Mercedes Lachy, Eric Scharf, Hulya Ulku, Craig W. Thorburn, and Eloy Vidal.

The team also thankfully acknowledges helpful comments and support from Jose Daniel Reyes, Daniel Lederman, Daniela Marrotta, David Gould, Desiree González, Cynthia Flores Mora, Patricia Chacon Holt, Patricia Mendez, Aleksandra Iwulska, and Sergio Vargas Tellez.

Special thanks to the Ministry of Foreign Trade (*Ministerio de Comercio Exterior* [COMEX]) for facilitating the preparatory mission for the report and for the support from its staff, especially Francisco Monge, Karen Chan, Reyner Brenes, Natalia Porras, Carolina Vargas, and Alejandra Aguilar. Furthermore, special thanks to the Costa Rican Investment Promotion Agency (*Coalición Costarricense de Iniciativas de Desarrollo* [CINDE]), which supported the survey of high-tech firms in the free trade zone (FTZ). Additional thanks to the various organizations that provide the data used in this report, including the Central Bank of Costa Rica, the Costa Rican Social Security Administration (*Caja Costarricense de Seguro Social* [CCSS]), Costa Rican Electricity Institute (ICE), National Institute of Statistics and Census (INEC), National Insurance Institute (INS), Center for Promotion of Foreign Trade (PROCOMER), *Radiográfica de Costa Rica* (RACSA), *Rectoría de Telecomunicaciones* (RETEL), Superintendency of Insurance (SUGESE), and Superintendency of Telecommunications (SUTEL).

The Multi-Donor Trust Fund for Trade provided financial support for this publication.

Contributors

About the Editors

Friederike (Fritzi) Koehler-Geib is a senior economist in the Macroeconomics and Fiscal Management global practice group in the Latin America Department of the World Bank in Washington, DC. Her prior work experience includes the Economic Policy and Debt department of the PREM network of the World Bank and the Monetary and Capital Markets department, as well as the Research Department of the International Monetary Fund. Her research interests fall in the area of international finance and international macroeconomics. She has written articles on financial crises and their contagion, the volatility of economic growth, fiscal policy, and asset management. Ms. Koehler-Geib holds a PhD in economics from Ludwig Maximilians University (Munich), with extended research stays at Universitat Pompeu Fabra (Barcelona) and two master's degrees, one from the University of St. Gallen, HEC Paris and one from the University of Michigan.

Susana M. Sanchez is a senior economist in the Macroeconomics and Fiscal Management global practice group of the World Bank. She has published several articles and reports covering a variety of development topics. Ms. Sanchez has worked on issues related to growth, poverty, investment climate, labor markets, and access to finance. She has a PhD in development economics and a master's degree in economics, both from the Ohio State University.

About the Authors

Alejandra Castro is an intellectual property partner at Arias & Muñoz, a Costa Rican law firm. She is an experienced attorney who has counseled numerous innovation entities on international trade and intellectual property-related issues and has actively participated in free trade agreement negotiations with the United States, Central America, and the Dominican Republic. She is an adviser to the World Intellectual Property Rights Organization, vice president of the Information Technology Chambers in Costa Rica, a member of the board of directors of the Audiovisual Industry Chamber, and president of the Information Technology Law Association. Ms. Castro obtained her law degree from the

University of Costa Rica and holds a PhD in constitutional law, with emphasis in information technology and a master's in information technology law, both from the Universidad Complutense de Madrid.

Mateo Clavijo is a PhD candidate at the Pompeu Fabra University in Spain. Previously, he was a research analyst at the Macro and Fiscal Management global practice of the World Bank. His research interests are in the areas of monetary economics, business cycles, and fiscal policy. Mr. Clavijo has a master's in economics from the University of Los Andes in Colombia.

Craig W. Thorburn is a lead insurance specialist at the World Bank. Since 2002, he has provided technical assistance, published research, and managed projects that enhance insurance market development, regulation, and supervisory capacity. He leads the World Bank representation on a number of International Association of Insurance Supervisors (IAIS) committees, including those directed at standard setting, establishing Insurance Core Principles, supporting implementation initiatives, and conducting peer assessments and reviews. Prior to joining the World Bank, he was a government actuary in Australia, Chief of Life Insurance Supervision, and a general manager in the Diversified Institutions Division of the Australian Prudential Regulation Authority, supervising a range of financial conglomerates. Mr. Thorburn qualified as an actuary in 1987 and is a member of both the Australian and North American Actuarial Associations.

Hulya Ulku is a senior economist at the Doing Business Unit, in the Development Economics Vice Presidency of the World Bank. Prior to joining the World Bank in 2013, she worked as a lecturer in development economics at the University of Manchester for nine years, where she directed the Development Economics and Policy master's program and taught international trade and macroeconomics courses to graduate students. She has published extensively on innovation and economic growth in developing and developed countries, as well as on the determinants and developmental potentials of remittances, international aid, and labor market regulations. Ms. Ulku holds a bachelor's degree in public finance from Gazi University (Ankara, Turkey) and a master's and PhD, both in economics, from Brandeis University (Waltham, Massachusetts).

Eloy Vidal is an experienced telecommunications consultant with previous managerial responsibility for several telecommunications public policy design, sector restructuring, privatization of state-owned enterprises, public-private partnerships, and telecommunications projects of the World Bank in Washington, DC. Mr. Vidal received a master of science in electrical engineering from Stanford University (California) in 1971 and an electrical engineering degree from Universidad de Costa Rica (San José) in 1968.

Abbreviations

ACAR	Costa Rican Association of Insurance and Reinsurance (*Asociación Costarricense de Aseguradores y Reaseguradores*)
ADSL	asymmetric digital subscriber line
ARESEP	Regulatory Authority of Public Services (*Autoridad Reguladora de los Servicios Públicos*)
ASSAL	Association of Insurance Supervisors of Latin America (*Asociación de Supervisores de Seguros de Latinoamérica*)
AXCO	Insurance Information Services
BCCR	Central Bank of Costa Rica
BSE	Uruguay's State Insurance Bank (*Banco de Seguros del Estado de Uruguay*)
CAFTA	Central America–United States Free Trade Agreement
CAFTA-DR	Dominican Republic–Central America–United States Free Trade Agreement
CBERA	Caribbean Basin Economic Recovery Act
CBI	Caribbean Basin Initiative
CBTPA	Caribbean Basin Trade Partnership Act
CCSS	Costa Rican Social Security Administration (*Caja Costarricense de Seguro Social*)
CINDE	Costa Rica Investment Promotion Agency (*Coalición Costarricense de Iniciativas de Desarrollo*)
COMEX	Ministry of Foreign Trade (*Ministerio de Comercio Exterior*)
CONASSIF	National Council for the Supervision of the Financial System (*Consejo Nacional de Supervisión del Sistema Financiero*)
CPI	consumer price index
CRC	Costa Rican colón
FDA	Food and Drug Administration
FDI	foreign direct investment
FONATEL	National Telecomunications Fund (*Fondo Nacional de Telecomunicaciones*)

FTA	free trade agreement
FTZ	free trade zone
GAM	Greater Metropolitan Area of the Central Valley of Costa Rica
GDP	gross domestic product
GVC	global value chains
HDI	Human Development Index
HSPA	High Speed Packet Access
ICE	Costa Rican Electricity Institute (*Instituto Costarricense de Electricidad*)
ICT	information and communication technology
IMF	International Monetary Fund
INEC	National Institute of Statistics and Census (*Instituto Nacional de Estadísticas y Censos*)
INS	National Insurance Institute (*Instituto Nacional de Seguros*)
IP	intellectual property
IT	information technology
ITU	International Telecommunication Union
KB	kilobyte
Kbps	kilobits per second
LRIC	long-term incremental costs
MB	megabyte
Mbps	megabits per second
MGPSP	Ministry of Interior, Justice and Public Security (*Ministerio de Gobernación, Justicia y Seguridad Pública*)
MICITT	Ministry of Science, Technology and Telecommunications (*Ministerio de Ciencia, Tecnología y Telecomunicaciones*)
MINAET	Ministry of Environment, Energy and Telecommunications (*Ministerio de Ambiente, Energía y Telecomunicaciones*)
MMS	multimedia messaging system
MNC	multinational company
MNVO	mobile network virtual operator
NAFTA	North American Free Trade Agreement
OECD	Organisation for Economic Co-operation and Development
OEM	original equipment manufacturer
OLS	ordinary least squares
ORBA	*Observatorio Regional de Banda Ancha* (Regional Broadband Observatory)
PAHO	Pan American Health Organization
PALIC	Pan American Life Insurance de Costa Rica

PROCOMER	Center for Promotion of Foreign Trade (*Promotora del Comercio Exterior*)
PRUGAM	Regional and Urban Plan for the Greater Metropolitan Area of the Central Valley of Costa Rica (*Planificación Regional y Urbana de la Gran Área Metropolitana del Valle Central de Costa Rica*)
RACSA	Radiográfica Costarricense, S.S.
RETEL	Telecommunications Rectory (*Rectoría de Telecomunicaciones*)
SMS	set number of minutes
SUGESE	Superintendency of Insurance (*Superintendencia General de Seguros*)
SUTEL	Superintendency of Telecommunications (*Superintendencia de Telecomunicaciones*)
TRIPS	Trade-Related Aspects of Intellectual Property Rights
VoIP	voice over Internet protocol
WDI	World Development Indicators
WHO	World Health Organization
WTO	World Trade Organization

Overview

Susana M. Sanchez and Friederike (Fritzi) Koehler-Geib

The Dominican Republic–Central America–United States Free Trade Agreement
(CAFTA-DR) has been fundamental in creating a stable framework for Costa
Rica's trade with the United States. On August 5, 2004, the United States
entered into a free trade agreement (FTA) with the Dominican Republic and five
Central American countries (Costa Rica, El Salvador, Guatemala, Honduras, and
Nicaragua). Following a national referendum in 2007, with 51.6 percent of
voters approving, Costa Rica ratified the treaty, which came into force on
January 1, 2009. The agreement consolidated benefits that had previously been
unilaterally extended under the Caribbean Basin Initiative (CBI) into a multilateral FTA, providing a much more stable environment for trade relationships,
although with limited changes to overall market access relative to the CBI.

For Costa Rica, CAFTA-DR is more than a trade agreement. Besides eliminating tariffs and reducing non-tariff barriers between member countries, CAFTA-DR
also introduced major changes to the legal framework of member countries,
reducing barriers to services, promoting transparency, and ensuring a secure and
predictable environment for investors. The most substantial transformation was
breaking down government monopolies in the telecommunications and insurance sectors. Legal changes increased the attractiveness of member countries to
foreign investors. The agreement provides protection for all forms of investment,
including enterprises, debt, concessions, contracts, and intellectual property (IP).
CAFTA-DR also meets the labor objectives set out by the U.S. Congress and
grants workers improved access to procedures that protect their rights. Moreover,
CAFTA-DR led to the modernization of key norms and procedures in areas such
as government procurement and IP rights.

This report analyzes how CAFTA-DR has impacted the Costa Rican economy
in the five years after ratification, both on a macro level and in key specific
sectors. The trade agreement was highly controversial in Costa Rica when it was
under negotiations, with some arguing that it would give the economy a major
boost and others suggesting that it would negatively impact specific sectors and
social groups. While recognizing the limitations of data and analysis on such a
complex issue in such a short time after coming into effect, this report seeks to

better understand what CAFTA-DR, and the legal changes that came along with it, has meant for Costa Rica. It presents stylized facts and some indication of the impact of CAFTA-DR, without claiming to establish a stringent causal link or being able to disentangle it fully from other effects. At the request of the Costa Rican government, the report considers impacts at both the macro level as well as in the specific sectors of the high-tech industry, telecommunications, insurance, and pharmaceuticals.

The report shows that CAFTA-DR is yielding benefits to the Costa Rican economy, but it is too early to provide a complete account after just five years. The agreement has succeeded to further trade integration between Costa Rica, the United States, and other CAFTA-DR countries. Exports to the United States began increasing several years before the agreement, but CAFTA-DR accelerated the trend. Costa Rica continues attracting foreign direct investment (FDI) above levels observed in other CAFTA-DR countries, with an increasing share from U.S. investors and a focus on medical devices and business services. An online survey and interviews of high-tech firms in free trade zones (FTZs) found that CAFTA-DR was an important factor in the investment decisions. CAFTA-DR ignited an explosion of changes in the telecom and insurance sectors, bringing new regulatory frameworks, competition, product innovations, and price reductions. Consumers are reaping the benefits of improved telecom and insurance services. But some issues remain for those markets to mature. Finally, the concern regarding the potential negative impact on the Costa Rican Social Security Administration's (CCSS) finances due to the IP rights measures has not been observed.

Trade and FDI Patterns

This section provides stylized facts on trade and FDI patterns over time. Multiple reasons make it difficult to establish a direct causal link between trade and FDI trends and CAFTA-DR, including the development trajectory of the country, domestic economic policies, multiple other trade agreements joined by Costa Rica before and after CAFTA-DR, and the intervening impact of the global economic crisis. Nevertheless, some trends are likely attributable to the trade agreement.

Costa Rica has experienced significant shifts in its trade flows over the past 20 years, with an overall increase in trade integration with the United States and Central America. A gravity model estimate of trade indicates that some of the increase in exports to the United States can be linked to CAFTA-DR, while the result is insignificant in the case of imports from the United States to Costa Rica.

Over the past two decades, the country has successfully moved up the global value chains. The share of traditional exports has declined in favor of non-traditional and higher value goods. Moreover, the share of electronic products and medical instruments and appliances in total exports has been constantly rising.

In terms of FDI, the country has been very successful, and the composition of the flows has changed considerably since CAFTA-DR, with an increasing share of investment in services. Since 2000, FDI to Costa Rica has ranged between 2.0

and 7.0 percent of gross domestic product (GDP), and stood at 5.1 percent in 2012. The share of FDI originating from the United States has remained high. A major shift since the signing and ratification of CAFTA-DR has been the increase in inflows into the services sector.

The High-Tech Sector: FDI and Export Performance

Although both FDI and exports of Costa Rica's high-tech industry have been trending steadily upward since the 1990s, CAFTA-DR is expected to contribute to further developments. The majority of multinational companies (MNCs) in the high-tech sector are from the United States, and the agreement was expected to strengthen the attractiveness of Costa Rica as a destination for foreign investors. Thus, a review of the FDI and export performance of high-tech sectors (electronics, medical instruments, and business service) can provide insights into the short-term impact of CAFTA-DR. The analysis is conducted in light of key historical developments shaping the high-tech sector (the launch of the FTZs in 1981; arrival of Intel in 1997; signing of CAFTA-DR in August 2004, followed by a referendum for its approval in 2007; and full commitment to CAFTA-DR in January 2009) and the fact that CAFTA-DR came into effect in the midst of the 2008/09 global financial crisis.

In spite of the adverse effects of the global financial crisis, the number of MNCs and the total amount of FDI inflows to Costa Rica increased significantly following the signing of CAFTA-DR in 2004 and its entry into force in 2009. The GDP share of total FDI inflows to Costa Rica increased substantially after 2004 until the onset of the global financial crisis, during which it dropped significantly, though the decline was still smaller than the regional average. This performance was most likely due to CAFTA-DR.

The FDI share of the electronics sector has been stagnant since 2004, while the share of medical devices and business services has been on an impressive upward path, especially after CAFTA-DR came into force in 2009. The rise in the FDI shares of medical devices appears to be a result of increased interest in the sector by U.S. companies following CAFTA-DR, while the rise in the FDI share of the business services sector appears to stem largely from the liberalization of the telecommunications sector due to CAFTA-DR.

Total export share of GDP increased steadily throughout the 1990s and most of the 2000s, with the largest increases taking place after the arrival of Intel in 1997 and the signing of CAFTA-DR in 2004, before declining since 2007. However, these aggregate figures mask some interesting changes in the composition of exports of high-tech industries. Although the export share of the electronics sector has remained largely flat throughout the 2000s, the export share of medical devices has increased steadily since 2007, and has not been significantly affected by the financial crisis, most likely due to the arrival of new U.S. companies in the industry after CAFTA-DR. In addition, the IT-enabled sector had the largest boom in its export share during the second half of the 2000s, with the biggest increase taking place after CAFTA-DR came into force.

Costa Rica Five Years after CAFTA-DR • http://dx.doi.org/10.1596/978-1-4648-0568-4

Online surveys and in-person structured interviews indicate that CAFTA-DR was an important factor in the investment decisions of a significant number of firms. One of the most important benefits of CAFTA-DR was to reinforce government commitment to liberal trade and FDI-friendly policies and to strengthen the legal framework on the rights of foreign investors. Other important outcomes included an increase in the competitiveness of the Costa Rican economy through several provisions of CAFTA-DR, including the liberalization of the telecommunications and insurance sectors, which increased the FDI and exports of the high-tech sector.

Given that CAFTA-DR is still new, and that it came into force in the middle of the global financial crisis, many of its anticipated effects will take longer to be realized. Having already achieved most of its early- to mid-developmental goals, Costa Rica's next challenge is to attract FDI at the high end of the production chain in order to increase the value added content of production, and to establish linkages between foreign investors and local suppliers in order to increase the absorptive capacity and innovation capability of the country.

In order for Costa Rica not to fall into the middle-income country trap, it must transform its economy from being a recipient of innovation to producing it. One way of achieving this, as the experiences of the Asian Tigers (Hong Kong SAR, China; Singapore; Republic of Korea, and Taiwan, China) have shown, is to maintain FDI and export-oriented policies—as Costa Rica has been successfully doing during the last three decades—and to strengthen the ability of the country to innovate through increased investment in education and infrastructure and through greater exposure to advanced technologies.

Insurance: The End of a Monopoly and a New Beginning for a Market

CAFTA-DR imposed significant change on the insurance sector. A new insurance law was required for the liberalized market, a supervisory authority needed to be established and developed to full functionality, and the National Insurance Institute (*Instituto Nacional de Seguros* [INS])—the existing monopoly insurer—needed to adjust to the new environment. Until liberalization, the life insurance sector had been merely nascent. While the non-life business showed a penetration above regional comparisons, it tended to follow international pricing cycles with some amplification.

Insurance premiums have grown in a healthy fashion since liberalization, particularly in the life sector. By 2012 written premiums for all classes of business totaled CRC 466.16 billion (US$924 million), which is already substantial compared to other CAFTA-DR countries. Non-life premiums represented 80 percent, which in local currency terms was an increase of just over 16 percent over 2011 figures. As would be expected, life insurance offered considerable potential for growth, as it was substantially underdeveloped at the time of liberalization.

The market composition in terms of insurers, market share, and product offerings is still developing. Twelve insurers are competing in the market. The market share of the INS has fallen to around 90 percent of the total market (including compulsory classes) and the Herfindahl index has fallen to 8,799 and 8,290 for life and non-life segments, respectively. The increased proportion of business represented by life insurance and the falling measure of auto insurance as a proportion of total non-life business are both indicators of a maturing market. Furthermore, the product mix for non-life is becoming more diverse, reducing the level of risk to insurers as they have a more diverse portfolio of risks.

The new entrants have overcome the initial costs of establishing operations, and innovations in distributions are likely to increase access to insurance products. Legally, intermediation can be conducted through either agents or brokers, both of which can be individuals or companies. To date, the Superintendency of Insurance (*Superintendencia General de Seguros* [SUGESE]) has registered large numbers of intermediaries: agency companies (63), individual agents (1,692), brokerage firms (17), and individual agents (177). In addition there were 49 distributors of mass-marketed insurances and two registered cross-border providers. Microinsurance policies (*Seguros autoexpedibles*) have promoted innovations in distributions through kiosks and through relationships with banks, retailers, and the post office.

The insurance sector is showing benefits through improved operating performance, solid growth, product innovation, and improved efficiency. Expense ratios have declined by 10 percent between 2010 and 2012, which can be attributed to the impact of competitive initiatives on expense control, innovation from new entrants, as well as economies naturally generated from increased market size. Moreover, a 20 percent increase in claims ratios (payouts as a proportion of premiums) demonstrates increased value for money.

The liberalization dynamics are very similar in terms of pace and progress compared to the other countries, but the complete benefits of the initiative are not yet fully captured. New market entrants are seeking to compete and innovate, while the incumbent is seeking to defend share and meet new market challenges. These dynamics include gradual, rather than dramatic, reduction in INS market share, overall sector growth, and faster growth in life insurance. There is still plenty of distance to travel, but early progress has yielded results and indicates what can be expected in the future. Improved value, innovation, and dynamism in the sector have already made a positive economic contribution; the natural process toward a final balance in competition in the market usually takes many more years, so these early benefits are the tip of the iceberg. The INS has shown a keen interest in being part of the innovations in the sector.

There are some areas that would be useful for policymakers to consider for the future. First, the liberalization of compulsory automobile and occupational-risk business will likely require specific attention from the SUGESE, particularly regarding adequate statistics for pricing and provisioning, and arrangements for the treatment of cases involving uninsured or unidentified motorists or employers. Second, the INS should expand cautiously into new business lines and new jurisdictions, and can benefit from the lessons of other entities that have tried and failed in similar endeavors. Finally, continued development of supervisory capacity will need to be an ongoing priority as the SUGESE staff continue to grow into their supervisory roles.

Telecommunications and the End of Another Monopoly

CAFTA-DR opened the door for private investments in the telecommunications sector. A new telecommunications law was required for the liberalized market; a new regulator, Superintendency of Telecommunications (*Superintendencia de Telecomunicaciones* [SUTEL]), needed to be established and to develop its functionality; and the Costa Rican Electricity Institute (*Instituto Costarricense de Electricidad* [ICE]), the existing monopoly provider, needed to adjust to the new environment. Until liberalization, ICE dominated the telecommunications sector. In this environment, there was a large unmet demand for mobile telephone services, prices for Internet access were very high, and the sector was supply-constrained.

The market has shown extraordinary price reductions and growth in access following CAFTA-DR. The forces of competition have led to an abundant supply of services, prices for Internet access fell dramatically, and Costa Ricans have responded by subscribing massively to the new services. New entrants have become established and are actively competing with the ICE, which is responding to the competitive landscape with its own strategies. All indicators demonstrate that after sector liberalization, Costa Rica is well positioned in comparison with Latin American countries of similar GDP per capita. Today consumers can buy a cell line instantly, without the long wait times prevalent prior to liberalization. Finally, the telecommunications sector's contribution to GDP increased substantially. The sector attracted large FDI flows, produced a large consumer surplus advantage stemming from reduced prices and increased Internet access and cellular lines, and made a large contribution to economic growth.

However, as in any liberalization of the telecommunications sector, some issues remain. In Costa Rica, these issues are partly due to the fact that the government still owns the largest telecommunications operator, which is not typical of the majority of Latin American countries. Four important challenges remain: liberalizing rates to allow for sufficient investment, broadening spectrum access to enable improved service, facilitating infrastructure sharing and municipal permits, and ensuring universal access by reforming the activities of the National Telecommunications Fund (*Fondo Nacional de Telecomunicaciones* [FONATEL]).

Intellectual Property Rights in CAFTA-DR and the Link to Pharmaceuticals in Costa Rica

The protection of IP was perhaps the most controversial aspect of CAFTA-DR. The CAFTA-DR's IP chapter is also the only one including regulations that could impact access to pharmaceuticals in Costa Rica. During discussions about the treaty, national opinion was divided between those who argued that IP regulations would lead to an increase in the price of medicines and those who believed that the provisions would incentivize innovative medicines to enter the market.

The local generic industry argued that IP provisions would prevent the approval of generic medicines and grant additional exclusive marketing rights to brand-name manufacturers. This led to concern that CAFTA-DR was going to severely restrict or block generic competition, leading to rising medicine prices and the disappearance of the generic market. The strongest position against IP rules held that these effects would make it economically unsustainable and legally impossible for the CCSS to ensure universal coverage and access to medicines for the population.

CAFTA-DR included provisions on IP rights. CAFTA-DR's ratification process actually led to the implementation of legislation sensitive to public health, adopted to avoid restrictions in the market for generic companies and to give flexibility to CCSS. The terms were as follows: (a) limiting patent term restoration to a maximum of 18 months; (b) a restrictive definition of innovative products limiting the scope of products subject to protection of test data; and (c) the preservation of provisions for parallel importation, compulsory licensing, and government use that were already part of Costa Rica's regulation prior to CAFTA-DR approval. CAFTA-DR expressly states that nothing in the agreement will affect a country's ability to take measures necessary to protect public health.

Despite discussions of the impact that IP provisions would have on the CCSS's financial results and access to generics, CAFTA-DR did not diminish the state's ability to fulfill its obligations to secure the right to health services of the Costa Rican population, as the following evidence indicates:

- About 8 percent of the CCSS's budget is used for medicine purchases.
- Most drugs developed and registered worldwide every year by pharmaceutical companies are new presentations or formulations of preexisting medicines, and only a small portion of these products are actually new chemical entities that could receive data protection according to Costa Rica's definition of new chemical entities.
- From 2009 to 2012, 2,541 new active ingredients were registered with the Ministry of Health, of which only 30 received data protection. Only one product with data protection is in the CCSS's Official Medicine List.
- Costa Rica has only granted patent linkage to four pharmaceutical products (or two active ingredients) registered at the Ministry of Health. This means that the marketing approval of generic drugs must await the expiration of the innovative drug's patent before producing those products.
- None of CAFTA-DR's provisions are actually affecting the CCSS's financial balance, and several studies confirm that the CCSS's financial crisis is not related to the cost of medicines. Analysis by the Pan American Health Organization (PAHO) of the current financial crisis at the CCSS showed that expenditures on medicines have not affected this situation.
- The CCSS has added seven active ingredients or 12 pharmaceutical presentations to its Official Medicine List. Only one product with data protection is included in the CCSS Official Medicine List (Tenofovir disoproxil fumarate). The IP rules have not restricted or blocked the purchase of generic products by the CCSS.

CHAPTER 1

The Context of CAFTA-DR in Costa Rica

Friederike (Fritzi) Koehler-Geib and Mateo Clavijo

Introduction

The Dominican Republic–Central America–United States Free Trade Agreement (CAFTA-DR), has been more than a trade agreement for Costa Rica, and for this reason it catalyzed intense debate about potential impacts on the economy. In particular, CAFTA-DR brought about the opening of state monopolies in telecommunications and insurance, which polarized the country. As a consequence, the agreement could only be ratified after narrowly passing a referendum in October 2007. Topics of debate included the impact on overall export and growth performance, on foreign direct investment (FDI) flows, and on sectors such as agriculture, industry, telecommunications, insurance, and health.

Given the high level of interest and controversy prior to CAFTA-DR's ratification, it is worth examining its actual impacts on the economy. The purpose of the current study is to take stock of these impacts, and to identify areas where complementary reform is needed to reap the full benefit of the agreement. Given that only five years have elapsed since ratification and some provisions are not in force yet (for example, those related to the agricultural sector), the establishment of causal links is beyond the scope of this analysis. Moreover, the coincidence of the ratification of CAFTA-DR with the global economic and financial crisis makes it difficult to identify the agreement's impact. Finally, disentangling the impact of CAFTA-DR from other free trade agreements (FTAs), such as the Caribbean Basin Initiative (CBI), is a challenge. The study presents stylized facts and some indication of the impact of CAFTA-DR, without claiming to establish a stringent causal link or being able to disentangle it fully from other effects.

This chapter provides the background of the agreement, setting the stage for the sector-specific assessments in subsequent chapters. The chapter first provides the historical context of the agreement, then gives an overview of the main arguments in favor of and against the agreement prior to its ratification, summarizes the main legal changes, and sketches an account of trade and FDI patterns.

CAFTA-DR in Historical Context

Costa Rica has used trade liberalization and promotion of international trade as a core development strategy for decades. As early as 1963, Costa Rica joined the General Treaty on Central American Economic Integration that had been initially signed by El Salvador, Guatemala, Honduras, and Nicaragua in 1960. This agreement spearheaded trade integration in Central America that has so far led to a customs union. Liberalizing the movement of workers across the member states is the component of a common market that is outstanding (O'Keefe 2009). CBI was an important step for Costa Rica's trade relationships with the United States. On August 5, 1983, the U.S. Congress passed the Caribbean Basin Economic Recovery Act (CBERA), a preferential trade and tax benefits program to support political and economic stability in 27 Caribbean countries and territories including Costa Rica (Dypski 2002).[1] This act was amended twice in 1990 and 2000, granting further benefits to the member countries. Due to the nature of this initiative, the U.S. Congress had to regularly ratify it and could cancel it or exclude countries at any point.[2] Through the CBI, Central America was subject to the same terms as Mexico for apparel, and duty-free access was given to approximately 75 percent of Central America's exports to the United States by 2000 (Lopez and Shankar 2011). Besides the CBI, Costa Rica signed a FTA with Canada primarily on the trade of goods, and became the first Central American country with an FTA with a developed economy when the agreement entered into force in 2002. In the same year, Costa Rica signed two more treaties with Chile and the Dominican Republic. Another instrument for trade policy have been the free trade zones (FTZs), which are an important vehicle for Costa Rica to attract FDI.

CAFTA-DR has been fundamental in creating a stable and reliable framework for Costa Rica's trade with the United States. On August 5, 2004, the United States entered into an FTA with the Dominican Republic and five Central American countries (Costa Rica, El Salvador, Guatemala, Honduras, and Nicaragua). The agreement consolidated benefits that had previously been extended on a unilateral basis under CBI into a multilateral FTA for the CAFTA-DR member states, providing a much more stable trade environment (Hornbeck 2012).

CAFTA-DR has led to the liberalization of the Costa Rican insurance and telecom sectors and the introduction of regulatory reforms. Regarding market access, CAFTA-DR generated limited changes relative to the arrangements under CBI. Some improvements over the CBI were made in the area of manufacturing, where additional tariffs were eliminated for a few products that had been explicitly excluded under CBI preferences, such as canned tuna, shoes, and jewelry. In agriculture, a reciprocal elimination of tariffs consolidated access previously allowed under CBI, and provided for some expansion of zero-duty access for a few new products that had been excluded from the preferences. However, those changes in agriculture were agreed with transition periods ranging from 5 to 20 years, depending on the goods, to allow for gradual adjustment (Jaramillo and Lederman 2006). In terms of textiles and apparel, CAFTA-DR implied increased flexibility in the rules of origin, which should allow zero-duty entry to the United States[3] The main changes occurred through domestic reforms, most importantly the liberalizations of the insurance and telecommunications markets, which will be discussed in further detail in subsequent chapters. In addition, key norms and procedures in areas such as government procurement, intellectual property rights, and the treatment of foreign investors were modernized under CAFTA-DR, and have the potential to improve the country's investment climate (Jaramillo and Lederman 2006).

Costa Rica was the last member country to ratify the agreement, following a referendum in October 2007. The U.S. Congress signed the bill to implement CAFTA-DR on July 28, 2005; CAFTA-DR entered into force in El Salvador on March 1, 2006; in Honduras and Nicaragua on April 1, 2006; in Guatemala on July 1, 2006; in the Dominican Republic on March 1, 2007; and in Costa Rica on January 1, 2009. The liberalization of the telecommunications and insurance sectors in Costa Rica required substantial legislative changes. This led to strong opposition to CAFTA-DR, both in the Costa Rican Legislative Assembly and by social and labor organizations, delaying ratification. In October 2007, the Costa Rican electorate narrowly approved the treaty in a referendum (51 percent of votes cast in favor and 48 percent against), enabling its entry into force at the beginning of 2009.

Encouraged by CAFTA-DR, Costa Rica entered into further FTAs. In 2011, Costa Rica signed and ratified an FTA with China that included raw materials, intermediate goods, and other merchandise, mainly electronics. Costa Rica entered into a regional FTA with El Salvador, Guatemala, Mexico, and Nicaragua, which was signed in 2011 and entered into force in Costa Rica in July 2013. In addition, Costa Rica signed separate FTAs with Peru and Singapore in 2011, entering into force in July and June 2013, respectively. Together with other Central American countries, Costa Rica also negotiated an association agreement with the European Union. As with most of the other trade agreements, the association agreement contains rules for raw materials, intermediate goods, and other merchandise, but also covers provisions for openness to European FDI in services such as telecommunications, clean technology, biotechnology, medical industry, and public infrastructure. The trade component of the agreement entered into force in October 1, 2013.

Economic Arguments for and against CAFTA-DR at the Time of Ratification

Given its comprehensive nature, CAFTA-DR sparked intense debate about its risks and benefits in Costa Rica. Because Costa Rica was the last country in Central America to eventually open up monopolies in telecommunications and insurance, the debate was particularly heated. Topics of discussion included the impact on overall export and growth performance; on FDI flows; and on sectors such as agriculture, industry, telecommunications, insurance, and health. While labor and environmental standards were also taken up both by supporters and opponents of the agreement, these topics are not addressed in this study.

Prior to the referendum, the debate about CAFTA-DR polarized Costa Rica, with a major concern that the agreement could harm the agricultural and industrial sectors. Opponents argued that the agreement would be asymmetrical and unfavorable for Costa Rica, due to U.S. agricultural subsidies, technological advantages, and market power. Opponents were concerned that the agreement would only generate benefits for large-scale agricultural corporations and already competitive industries, while harming small farmers and other small and medium-sized enterprises. With CAFTA-DR, it was feared that small farmers would not be able to compete with highly subsidized U.S. agricultural exports, and that small companies would be driven out of business, causing job losses (Public Broadcasting Service 2005; Reuters 2007).

Another concern resulted from the opening of government-run telecommunications and insurance monopolies. While CAFTA-DR did not require privatizing the state-run telecommunications and insurance companies, it led to the opening of both sectors. Strong public sector unions were concerned about job losses and argued that services could become more expensive for consumers (Latin Business Chronicle 2007). In the case of telecommunications, opponents of CAFTA-DR argued that private companies would enter into the most lucrative segments of the market, such as Internet services; this in turn was presented as a threat to the ability of the state-owned telecommunications provider, the Costa Rican Electricity Institute (*Instituto Costarricense de Electricidad* [ICE]) to subsidize losses in less profitable segments of the market, particularly rural and poor areas (Bindman 2008).

A third cluster of arguments against the agreement grouped around intellectual property rights and fears that strengthening regulations on these would negatively impact the public health care system. In particular, opponents argued that stricter rules regarding patent protection would slow down the entry of generic medicines into the Costa Rican market and consequently drive up prices for medicines. This would in turn harm the provision of services by the Costa Rican Social Security Administration (*Caja Costarricense de Seguro Social* [CCSS]), which serves 90 percent of the population (Latin Business Chronicle 2007).

The main arguments in favor of CAFTA-DR were the stable environment for trade with the United States and Central American neighbors and the potentially positive impacts on FDI and export flows. Supporters of CAFTA-DR brought forward general arguments in favor of FTAs, such as the positive effects on FDI flows of lowering tariffs, expanding market size, reallocating resources efficiently, increasing economies of scale, promoting technology diffusion, and protecting intellectual property rights. In addition, they argued that the new multilateral agreement would generate legal certainty, in contrast to the CBI, which could be removed by the U.S. Congress at any point (Hornbeck 2012;

Latin Business Chronicle 2007). Moreover, proponents pointed out that the other Central American countries had already ratified the agreement and that Costa Rica would lose part of its competitive edge compared with those countries (Lydersen 2007). A further argument in favor of the agreement was that the potentially improved provision of telecommunications and insurance services in a competitive environment, along with improved regulatory processes and the legal certainty of a multinational trade agreement with the United States, would attract more FDI to Costa Rica and would ultimately help the country move toward the production of higher-value goods and bolster its export and growth performance (Latin Business Chronicle 2007).

Proponents argued that impacts on the industrial and agricultural sectors would be mainly positive due to adjustments in the sectors already having occurred prior to CAFTA-DR and the emergence of new opportunities. In particular, supporters of the agreement referred to anecdotal evidence from other CAFTA-DR countries that had already ratified the agreement, presenting positive impacts on industry and small businesses; these benefited more from FTAs than large corporations, which did not need FTAs to be competitive in international markets (Murphy 2007). Moreover, backers argued that small business owners would not suffer under CAFTA-DR due to wider lines of products to import, export, and distribute. Another argument pertaining to agriculture was that Costa Rica's transformation had already started over the 25–30 years prior to the negotiations of CAFTA-DR on the back of the country's structural adjustment plans. In that time, agricultural production had shifted from rice, beans, and yellow corn for domestic consumption to highly successful production for export of pineapples, melons, strawberries, winter vegetables, and similar crops. Therefore, only a modest further adjustment in the sector was expected (Latin Business Chronicle 2007).

A third set of arguments in favor of CAFTA-DR related to efficiency gains and benefits to consumers due to potentially lower prices and better service provision. The argument of lower prices and better service was particularly prominent in telecommunications and insurance, where supporters of CAFTA-DR argued that the liberalization and competition would force state-owned companies to operate more efficiently (Roberts and Markheim 2007).

Overall, research suggests that complementary reforms are needed to reap the full benefits of CAFTA-DR. In the case of Central America, Lopez and Shankar (2011) identify infrastructure reforms (differentiating between energy and logistics and transportation), human capital, access to finance, competition policy, and enforcement of intellectual property rights as important complements. With specific attention to Costa Rica, Jaramillo and Lederman (2006) mention improving road quality, enhancing port and customs efficiency, boosting financial depth, and improving the quality and coverage of secondary education.

The jury is still out on most of the arguments for or against the agreement, and the current study intends to provide stylized facts and an initial analysis to serve as a starting point for discussion about the impact of CAFTA-DR so far.

While the study can offer an overview of trends and a stylized narrative, rigorous disentanglement of causal effects and attribution of effects exclusively to CAFTA-DR is not possible, due to the relatively short time period that has elapsed since its entry into force and the difficulty of measuring the impact of CAFTA-DR relative to the impact of the international financial crisis and the role of previous and subsequent trade agreements.

Legal and Regulatory Changes with CAFTA-DR

CAFTA-DR led to a major adjustment of the legal system in a short time, both through substantial transformations and less fundamental amendments. The most sweeping legal transformations were the opening of the telecommunications and insurance markets. Other amendments updated and modernized Costa Rica's legislation without representing a radical overhaul, mainly in the areas of (a) intellectual property, (b) government procurement, (c) protection to distributors and agents of foreign companies, and (d) financial services. In these cases, the amendments would likely have taken place without the agreement, as they had been started before the negotiations, but CAFTA-DR accelerated their approval and implementation. Implementing CAFTA-DR in Costa Rica required approving 13 laws and adopting approximately 30 executive decrees or resolutions (see appendix A). While Costa Rica has generally complied with the legal requirements of CAFTA-DR within the agreed timeframe, in a few cases delays have occurred, mainly in telecommunications and insurance partly attributed to the time that elapsed before the referendum.

In a series of changes to the legal framework for the telecommunications sector, the government opened three market segments, mandated the modernization of ICE, established and clarified supervision, and enacted corresponding regulations. In June 2008, the Legislative Assembly approved the Telecommunications Law (*Ley General de Telecomunicaciones*), which opened private network services, Internet services, and mobile wireless services for competition. In addition, the so-called ICE Law (*Ley de Fortalecimiento y Modernización de las Entidades Públicas del Sector Telecomunicaciones*) approved in August of the same year modernized ICE and its subsidiaries with legislation to enable it to adapt to any changes in the legal regime of generation and delivery of electricity, telecommunications, info-communications, and other information services. The same law established the Superintendency of Telecommunications (*Superintendencia de Telecomunicaciones* [SUTEL]), which is responsible for regulating, implementing, monitoring, and controlling the telecommunications regulatory framework. Finally, several regulations were issued by the Regulatory Authority for Public Services of Costa Rica and through executive decrees. By the end of 2008, the relevant legislation and regulation was in place, albeit after the deadlines established under CAFTA-DR.

Main legal changes in the insurance sector included the establishment of a regulatory body and the opening of all insurance products. A major step in the opening of the insurance sector was the approval of the Insurance Law (*Ley Reguladora del*

Mercado de Seguros), which was approved in August 2008. This new law established the general framework for carrying out insurance activities in Costa Rica, as well as the obligation for insurers, producers, local service providers, and cross-border providers to register with or be licensed by the local regulator. It also created the Superintendency of Insurance (*Superintendencia General de Seguros* [SUGESE]) the local authority in charge of regulating the market, supervising its participants, and protecting consumers. Through the approval of the new law, Costa Rica covered the requirements under CAFTA-DR and also set up the regulatory apparatus needed to implement the new legislation.

Less fundamental legal amendments related to intellectual property and procurement. Intellectual property legislation was amended through, among others, the ratification of international agreements. Not all of the international agreements mentioned in CAFTA-DR have been ratified to date. The overall purpose of the changes is to render intellectual property protection more stringent. Procurement legislation in Costa Rica was amended to comply with obligation under CAFTA-DR regarding the integrity of procurement practices. The changes included the punishment of fraudulent procurement practices, including corruption, and an update of regulations to reflect specific procurement procedures, practices, and guidelines.

Trade and FDI Patterns with CAFTA-DR

The purpose of this section is to provide an overview of trade patterns over time, although establishing clear causality behind these trends is not possible. Several reasons make it difficult to establish a causal link. First of all, CAFTA-DR was only ratified in 2009, and some of its provisions have not been applied yet (for example, tariffs on agricultural goods). Second, as the changes in market access under CAFTA-DR were of secondary importance, it is difficult to disentangle the impact of the other elements. Third, CAFTA-DR was negotiated with the CBI and FTZs already in place, further complicating attempts to assign responsibility for impacts. Finally, identification of a causal link is handicapped by the fact that the global financial and economic crisis coincided with the ratification of CAFTA-DR. Despite all these caveats, some changes in trends are worth presenting. Although a causal link cannot be clearly established, these patterns are consistent with the theory that CAFTA-DR has already had a significant positive impact on trade.

Costa Rica has experienced significant shifts in its trade flows over the past 20 years, with an overall increase in trade integration with the United States and Central America. After growing continuously since the 1980s, Costa Rica's trade flows to the United States have increased significantly since the ratification of CAFTA-DR in the beginning of 2009, growing by around 50 percent by 2012 (see figure 1.1). Import growth from the United States to Costa Rica has been more moderate, amounting to almost 30 percent between 2008 and 2012, while the share of U.S. exports in Costa Rican GDP has actually declined by 3 percentage points of GDP over the same period, according to the International Monetary

Figure 1.1 Costa Rican Exports (FOB) to the United States, 2002–12

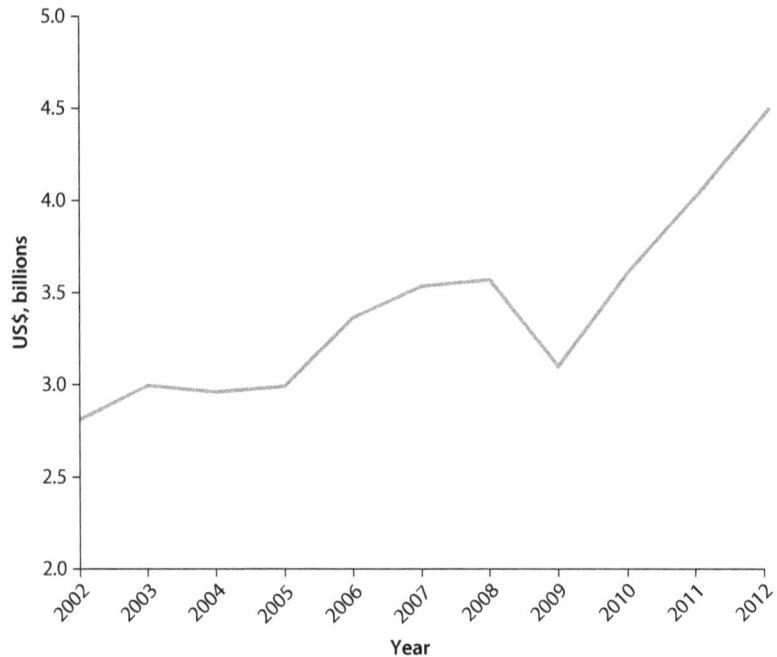

Source: Based on data from the Ministry of Foreign Trade (*Ministerio de Comercio Exterior* [COMEX]).
Note: FOB = free on board.

Fund (IMF). Costa Rica has increased its share of trade exports to Central America in total exports since the 1980s, while shares of exports to the United States and to the rest of the world have decreased (see appendix B). Costa Rica has also diversified imports away from the United States, with the share of U.S. imports in total imports dropping from 51 percent in 1980 to 34 percent in 2012, and the shares of the rest of Central America and of the rest of the world increasing.

Costa Rica seems to have benefited more than its Central American neighbors since 2009 in terms of commerce with the United States. Comparing U.S. imports from different Central American countries, Costa Rica displays by far the largest increase since 2009 (see figure 1.2). According to data from the Direction of Trade Statistics, the value of U.S. imports from Costa Rica tripled by 2012 compared to 2008, while the increases were more moderate for other Central American countries, varying between 10 and 60 percent.

A gravity model of trade suggests that some of the increase in exports of goods to the United States can be linked to CAFTA-DR, while the agreement had a statistically insignificant causal link with imports.[4] Following the methodology applied in Gould (1998), the current study applies the gravity model to a case of bilateral trade flows between Costa Rica and the United States using a time series sample in order to determine the effects of CAFTA-DR on exports and imports between Costa Rica and the United States. As the physical distance between

Figure 1.2 U.S. Imports (CIF) from CAFTA-DR Countries, 1980–2012

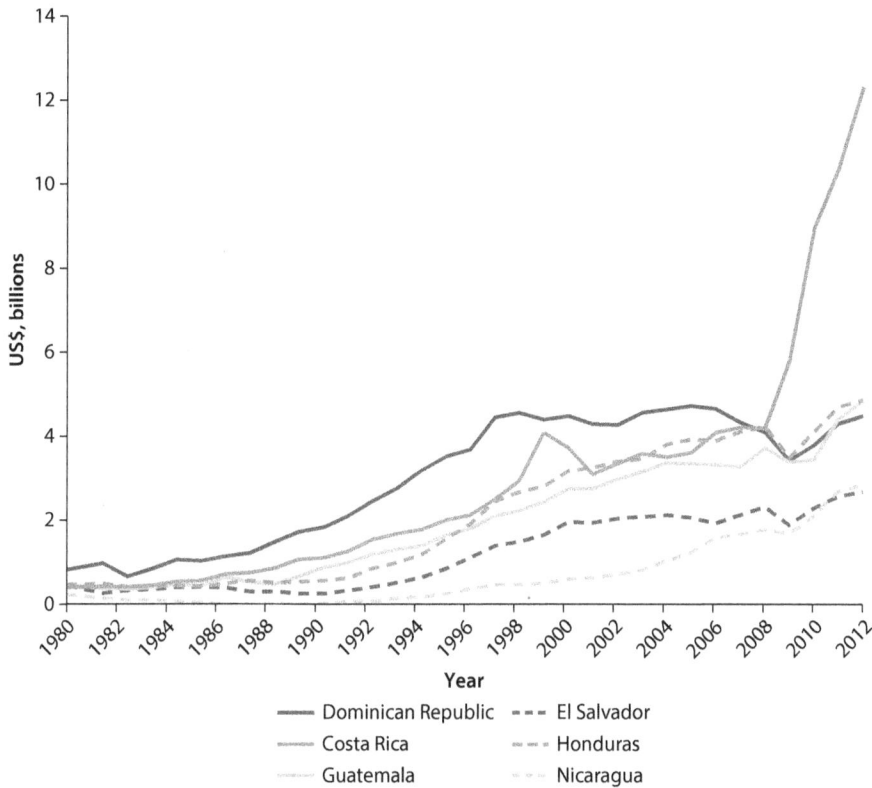

Source: Based on data from Direction of Trade Statistics, International Monetary Fund (IMF).
Note: Data of figures 1.1 and 1.2 are not comparable because of the different treatment of the value of intellectual property rights and exports from free trade zones. The Direction of Trade Statistics data are used for figure 1.2 as they are comparable across countries. CIF = cost, insurance, and freight.

Costa Rica and the United States does not vary over time, the measure of "distance" is not included in the underlying model for this study. Exports to the United States are estimated to have grown faster than they would have had there not been a FTA (see figure 1.3). This result is highly significant and not negligible in size. Similarly, imports from the United States are estimated to have grown faster than they would have had there not been a FTA (see figure 1.4). However, the estimation output shows this effect to be statistically insignificant. While these results indicate a link between CAFTA-DR and the increase in export flows toward the United States, the difficulties in identifying and disentangling the economic effects of the agreement have to be taken into account. Appendix C provides a detailed description of the gravity model.

Costa Rican export goods have successfully moved up the global value chain over the past two decades. An important shift occurred at the end of the 1990s, when the existing law on FTZs was amended. While prior to this change traditional exports (coffee, bananas, meat, and sugar) had represented around

Figure 1.3 Costa Rican Quarterly Exports to the United States, 1997–2012

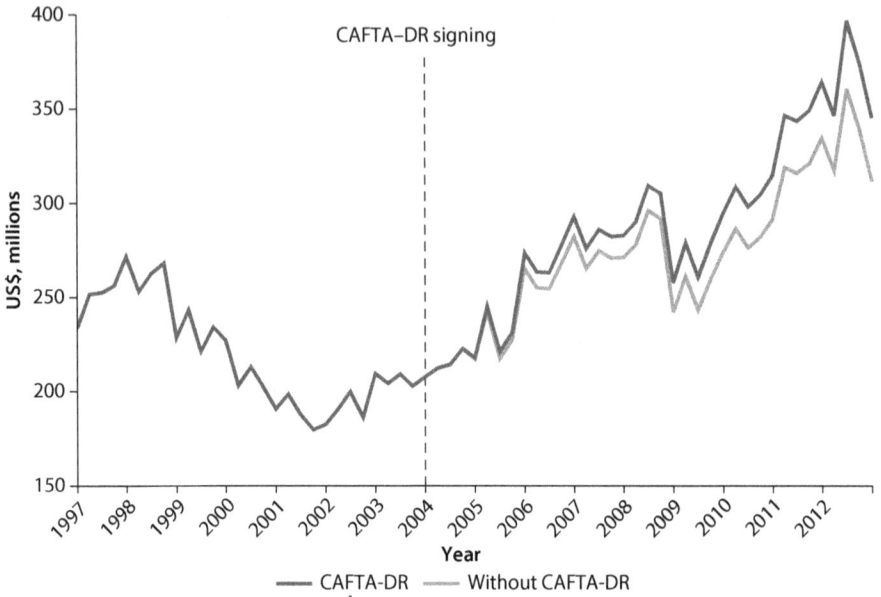

Sources: Based on data from Central Bank of Costa Rica (BCCR), Bureau of Economic Analysis, and the National Institute of Statistics and Census (*Instituto Nacional de Estadísticas y Censos* [INEC]). See appendix C for details.
Note: The data exclude exports from the free trade zones.

Figure 1.4 Costa Rican Quarterly Imports from the United States, 1997–2012

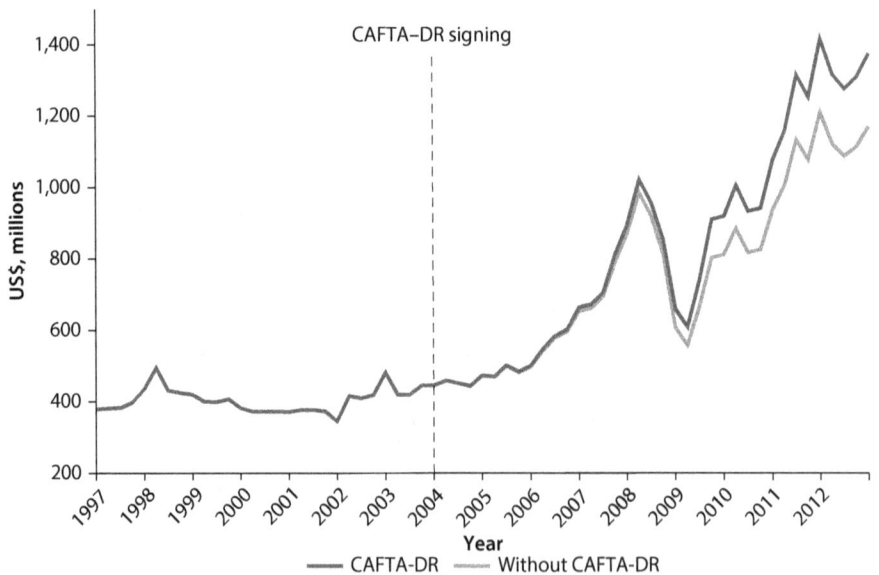

Source: Based on data from Central Bank of Costa Rica (BCCR), Bureau of Economic Analysis, and the National Institute of Statistics and Census (*Instituto Nacional de Estadísticas y Censos* [INEC]). See appendix C for details.
Note: The data exclude exports from the free trade zones.

Costa Rica Five Years after CAFTA-DR • http://dx.doi.org/10.1596/978-1-4648-0568-4

Figure 1.5 Composition of Total Exports of Costa Rican Goods (FOB), 1997–2013

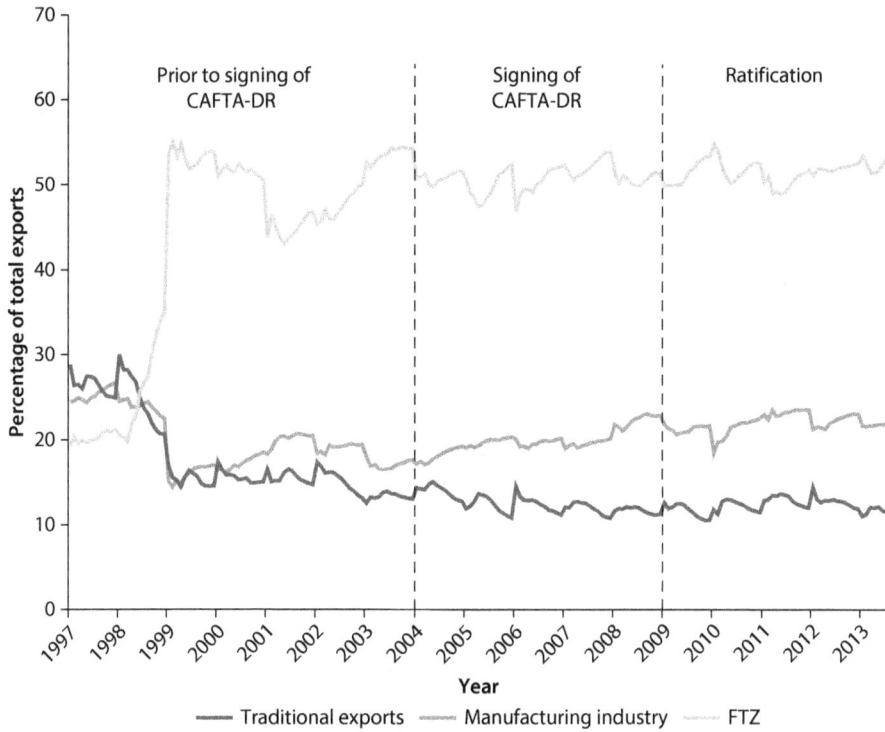

Source: Based on data from Central Bank of Costa Rica (BCCR).
Note: FOB = free on board; FTZ = free trade zone.

30 percent of total exports in 1997 and non-traditional exports (the manufacturing industry and products exported from FTZs) represented 24 percent and 20 percent of total exports, the share of products from FTZs increased to 54 percent after the amendment (see figure 1.5). This suggests a move toward higher-value exports. A similar trend can be seen between 2003 and 2012, with the share of electronic products and medical instruments and appliances consistently rising (see table 1.1).

At the same time the share of Costa Rica's top 20 export products has slightly decreased as the variety of products to the United States grew since 2003. The share of the top 5, top 10, and top 20 export products have remained fairly stable since 2003, with the percentage trending slightly downward (see table 1.1). An index of export concentration as measured by the share of agricultural products in total Costa Rican exports relative to the world average of the share of agricultural products in total exports indicates a drop in the concentration of Costa Rican exports over the longer term, with the most important decrease in concentration at the end of the 1990s. However, the data shows a slight increase since 2009 (see figure 1.6).[5] Moreover, the overall variety of products exported to the United States rose since 2003.

Table 1.1 Top Export Products, Percentage of Total Exports, 2003–12

2003		2005		2009		2012	
Product	% of total	Product	% of total	Product	% of total	Product	% of total
Parts and accessories (other than covers, carrying cases, and the like)[a]	24	Electronic integrated circuits and microassemblies	11	Parts and accessories (other than covers, carrying cases, and the like)[a]	13	Electronic integrated circuits and microassemblies	19
Bananas, including plantains, fresh or dried	10	Parts and accessories (other than covers, carrying cases, and the like)*	9	Electronic integrated circuits and microassemblies	10	Instruments and appliances used in medical, surgical, dental, or veterinary sciences	9
Instruments and appliances used in medical, surgical, dental, or veterinary sciences	8	Instruments and appliances used in medical, surgical, dental, or veterinary sciences	7	Instruments and appliances used in medical, surgical, dental, or veterinary sciences	8	Dates, figs, pineapples, avocados	7
Dates, figs, pineapples, avocados	3	Bananas, including plantains, fresh or dried	7	Dates, figs, pineapples, avocados	7	Bananas, including plantains, fresh or dried	6
Medicines	3	Dates, figs, pineapples, avocados	5	Bananas, including plantains, fresh or dried	7	Coffee, whether or not roasted	4
Top 5 in total exports	48		39		45		45
Top 10 in total exports	59		52		60		56
Top 20 in total exports	69		64		71		66

Source: Based on data from World Integrated Trade Solution.
a. Refers to parts and accessories suitable for use solely or principally with specific machines (headings 84.69–84.72).

Costa Rica has been very successful in attracting FDI, and the composition of the flows has changed considerably since CAFTA-DR. Since 2000, FDI to Costa Rica has ranged between 2 and 7 percent of GDP. In 2003, the year prior to the signing of CAFTA-DR, FDI stood at US$575 million (3.3 percent of GDP). There were slight increases in this percentage prior to the ratification of the FTA in 2009, and FDI reached 5.1 percent of GDP in 2012. Costa Rica's FDI inflows have historically come to a large extent from the United States. In 2000, these FDI inflows represented 75 percent of total FDI inflows. The U.S. share of FDI inflows has remained high with the ratification of CAFTA-DR, but has varied (see figure 1.7). An interesting pattern is the shift in composition of FDI since the ratification of CAFTA-DR. Before 2004, FDI in the service sector represented only 2 percent of total FDI inflows. In 2009 this increased to 18 percent of total FDI, and then further to 39 percent in 2012 after ratification and the liberalization of telecommunications and insurance sectors (see figure 1.8). Chapter 2 will provide an in-depth analysis of FDI flows in the high-tech sector.

Figure 1.6 Costa Rican Export Concentration Index of Agricultural Goods Relative to World Average, 1994–2011

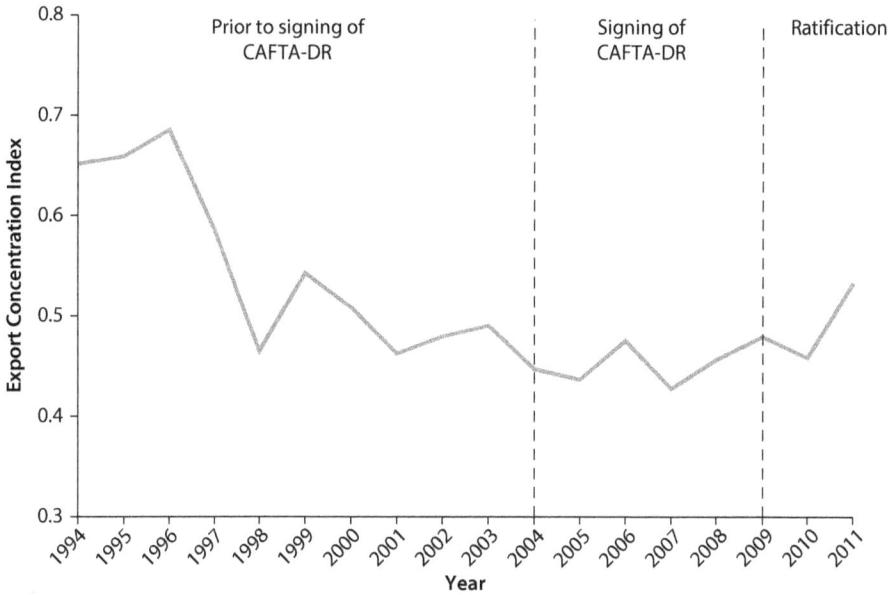

Source: Based on data from World Integrated Trade Solution.

Figure 1.7 FDI Inflows to Costa Rica by Country of Origin, 1997–2012

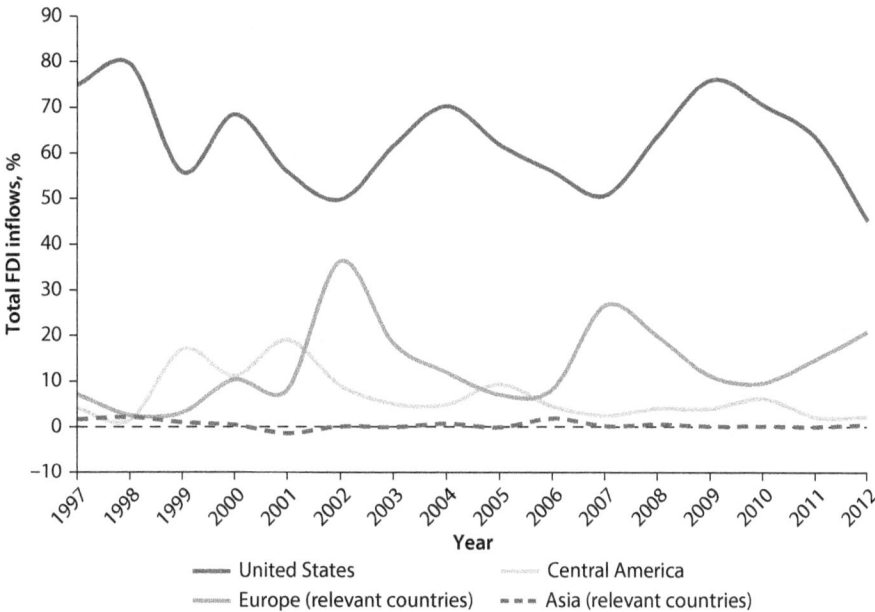

Source: Based on data from Central Bank of Costa Rica (BCCR).
Note: FDI = foreign direct investment.

Costa Rica Five Years after CAFTA-DR • http://dx.doi.org/10.1596/978-1-4648-0568-4

Figure 1.8 FDI Inflows to Costa Rica by Sector, 2004 versus 2012
% total FDI inflows

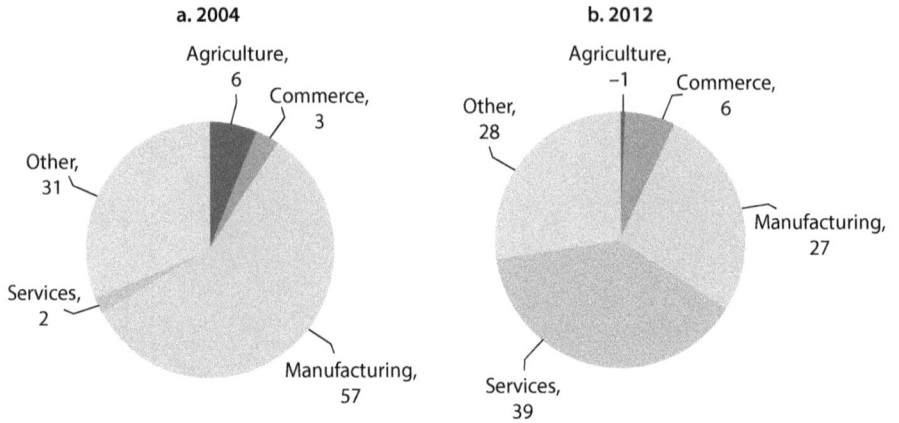

a. 2004

Agriculture,
6
Commerce,
3
Other,
31
Services,
2
Manufacturing,
57

b. 2012

Agriculture,
−1
Commerce,
6
Other,
28
Manufacturing,
27
Services,
39

Source: Based on data from the Central Bank of Costa Rica (BCCR).
Note: FDI = foreign direct investment.

Notes

1. The initial beneficiary economies included Anguilla, Antigua and Barbuda, The Bahamas, Barbados, Belize, British Virgin Islands, Cayman Islands, Costa Rica, Dominica, the Dominican Republic, El Salvador, Grenada, Guatemala, Guyana, Haiti, Honduras, Jamaica, Montserrat, Netherlands Antilles, Nicaragua, Panama, St. Kitts and Nevis, St. Lucia, St. Vincent and the Grenadines, Suriname, Trinidad and Tobago, and the Turks and Caicos Islands.

2. The Caribbean Basin Economic Recovery Expansion Act (CBERA) of 1990 (CBI II) was enacted under the Customs and Trade Act of 1990. CBI II amended CBERA by making its trade benefits permanent through the repeal of its 12-year termination date (initially set for September 30, 1995) and implementing certain improvements to its trade and tax benefits. The Caribbean Basin Trade Partnership Act (CBTPA), enacted on May 17, 2000, under the Trade and Development Act of 2000, reduces or eliminates tariffs and abolishes most quantitative restrictions on certain products that were previously not eligible for preferential treatment under either CBERA or CBI II. CBTPA is also intended to foster increased opportunities for U.S. companies in the textile and apparel sector to expand coproduction arrangements with countries in the CBI region. CBTPA benefits are in effect during a "transition period" that continues through September 30, 2010, or the date, if sooner, on which the Free Trade Area of the Americas or another free trade agreement as described in legislation enters into force between the United States and a CBTPA beneficiary country. As of 2013, there are 19 CBERA beneficiary countries as reported by the International Trade Administration.

3. Jaramillo and Lederman (2006) provide a concise summary of the changes of these sectors under CAFTA-DR.

4. The gravity model was based on export and import data from the Central Bank of Costa Rica, which excludes exports from free trade zones (FTZs). Therefore, the dataset is not comparable to the other data sources used in this first chapter of the report. The reason for using Central Bank data is that free trade zones house

companies with foreign and U.S. ownership. Finding an effect in a dataset excluding these zones is therefore a stricter test on the impact of CAFTA-DR.

5. This is defined as $DXi = (sum\ |hij - hj|) / 2$, where hij is the share of commodity j in the total exports of country i and hj is the share of the commodity j in world exports. The lower this index, the more diversified a country's exports.

References

Bindman, S. 2008. "Contentious CAFTA—A Turning Point for Costa Rica?" April 24. http://www.coha.org/contentious-cafta-a-turning-point-for-costa-rica/.

Dypski, M. 2002. "The Caribbean Basin Initiative: An Examination of Structural Dependency, Good Neighbor Relations, and American Investment." *Journal of Transnational Law and Policy* 12 (1): 95–136.

Gould, D. 1998. "Has NAFTA Changed North American Trade?" *Federal Reserve Bank of Dallas Economic Review* First Quarter: 12–23.

Hornbeck, J. 2012. *The Dominican Republic-Central America-United States Free Trade Agreement (CAFTA-DR): Developments in Trade and Investment.* Washington, DC: Congressional Research Services Report for Congress.

Jaramillo, F., and D. Lederman. 2006. *Challenges of CAFTA: Maximizing the Benefits for Central America.* Directions in Development Trade. Washington, DC: World Bank.

Latin Business Chronicle. 2007. "CAFTA's Impact on Costa Rica." October 15. http://www.latinbusinesschronicle.com/app/article.aspx?id=1705.

Lopez, H., and R. Shankar, eds. 2011. *Getting the Most Out of Free Trade Agreements in Central America.* Washington, DC: World Bank.

Lydersen, K. 2007. "Referendum in Costa Rica: Countdown to CAFTA?" September 27. http://upsidedownworld.org/main/trade-archives-54/912-karis-cafta-cr-article.

Murphy, J. 2007. "Costa Rica's CAFTA Choice—CAFTA Will Open Doors for Costa Rica's Workers, Farmers and Entrepreneurs." October 1. http://www.latinbusinesschronicle.com/app/article.aspx?id=1674.

O'Keefe, T. 2009. *Latin America and Caribbean Trade Agreements: Keys to a Prosperous Community of the Americas.* The Netherlands: Martinus Nijhoff.

Public Broadcasting Service. 2005. "Debating the Central American Free Trade Act." March 11. http://www.pbs.org/now/politics/caftadebate.html.

Reuters. 2007. "U.S. Trade Pact Is Protested in Costa Rica." *The New York Times,* October 7. http://www.nytimes.com/2007/10/01/world/americas/01costarica.html?_r=0.

Roberts, J. M., and D. Markheim. 2007. "Costa Rica and CAFTA: Chavista Rhetoric Threatens Trade Deal's Benefits." *Trade and Economic Freedom.* WebMemo #1656. http://www.heritage.org/research/reports/2007/10/costa-rica-and-cafta-chavista-rhetoric-threatens-trade-deals-benefits.

CHAPTER 2

CAFTA-DR and the High-Tech Sector: FDI and Export Performance

Hulya Ulku

Introduction

Free trade agreements (FTAs) are generally considered to promote foreign direct investment (FDI) and increase exports of member countries. They do so by lowering tariffs, expanding market size, reallocating resources efficiently, increasing economies of scale, and promoting technology diffusion. Most FTAs have provisions governing investment to reduce risk of expropriation and to ensure against the discrimination of foreign firms, further stimulating FDI inflows. FTAs also help governments lock in reforms, promoting stability and reassuring foreign investors about the security of their long-term investments. Moreover, given that most multinational companies (MNCs) operate in global value chains (GVCs), they are expected to increase the exports of the host countries and incorporate local suppliers, promoting their know-how and technological progress.

The Dominican Republic–Central America–United States Free Trade Agreement (CAFTA-DR) is of great significance for Costa Rica's long-term strategy of attracting more FDI and promoting export-based development. While the country has progressed significantly in diversifying output and exports away from traditional goods to manufacturing products, Costa Rica must further increase the high technology content of its manufacturing production and exports by attracting FDI in the high-end manufacturing sector and by increasing the links of MNCs to the local producers. Given that the majority of the MNCs in the high-tech sector are from the United States, and coupled with Costa Rica's attractive location and small size, CAFTA-DR can help the country achieve its goals.

This chapter analyzes the potential impact of CAFTA-DR on FDI and export performance of high-tech sectors in Costa Rica. The high-tech sectors included are electronics, medical instruments, and business services. The analysis uses secondary sources as well as primary data collected through two surveys from firms in the high-tech sector: an online survey of 61 firms, and in-depth interviews focusing on 11 firms. Furthermore, the analysis is conducted with attention to key historical developments shaping the high tech sector (for example, the launch of the free trade zones [FTZs] in 1981; the arrival of Intel in 1997; signing of CAFTA-DR in August 2004, followed by a referendum for its approval in 2007; and its ratification in January 2009) and the fact that CAFTA-DR came into effect in the midst of the 2008–09 global financial crisis. During that period most economies in the world suffered significant losses, which impacted the way in which CAFTA-DR had an effect on the Costa Rican economy. Given that CAFTA-DR came into force just five years ago, the analysis can provide insights only into the short-term impact of CAFTA-DR on Costa Rica's high-tech sector.

The findings provide interesting insights into the links between CAFTA-DR and the high-tech sector, which are summarized as follows:

- In spite of the adverse effects of the global financial crisis, the number of MNCs and total FDI inflows to Costa Rica increased significantly following the signing of CAFTA-DR in 2004 and its ratification in 2009. GDP share of total FDI inflows to Costa Rica also increased substantially after 2004 until the onset of the global financial crisis, during which it dropped significantly, though the decline was still smaller than the regional average, most likely due to CAFTA-DR.

- The FDI share of the electronics sector has been stagnating since 2004, while the share of medical devices and business services has been on an impressive upward path, especially after CAFTA-DR came into force in 2009. The rise in the FDI shares of the medical device industry appears to be a result of increased interest in the sector by U.S. companies following CAFTA-DR, while the rise in the FDI share of the business services sector appears to stem largely from the liberalization of the telecommunications sector, which is also due to CAFTA-DR.

- Although FDI inflows to Costa Rica from almost all source countries increased after CAFTA-DR in absolute terms, with the largest increase from the United States, only the United States, the Latin American region, and Mexico have increased their shares of total FDI following the agreement.

- Total exports as a share of GDP increased steadily throughout the 1990s and most of the 2000s, with the largest increases taking place after the arrival of Intel in 1997 and the signing of CAFTA-DR in 2004, before declining since 2007. However, these aggregate figures mask interesting changes in the composition of the exports of the high-tech industries. Although the export share of the electronics sector remained largely the same throughout the 2000s, the export share of medical devices has grown steadily since 2007 and has not been significantly affected by the financial crisis, most likely due to the arrival of new American companies in the industry after CAFTA-DR. In addition, the information technology (IT)–enabled sector had the largest boom in its export share during the second half of the 2000s, with the biggest increase taking place after CAFTA-DR came into force.

- Survey and interview evidence suggests that CAFTA-DR was an important factor in the investment decisions of a significant number of firms. One of the most important benefits of CAFTA-DR for foreign investors was to reinforce the government's commitment to liberal trade and FDI-friendly policies, and to strengthen the legal framework protecting the rights of foreign investors. Other important outcomes were an increase in the competitiveness of the Costa Rican economy through several provisions of CAFTA-DR, including the liberalization of the telecommunications and insurance sectors.

- Given that CAFTA-DR is still new and that it came into force in the middle of the global financial crisis, many of its anticipated effects will take some time to be realized. Costa Rica's next challenge is to attract FDI at the high end of the production chain in order to increase the value added content of production taking place in Costa Rica, and to establish links between foreign investors and local suppliers to increase the absorptive capacity and innovation capability.

- In order for Costa Rica not to fall into the middle-income country trap, it must transform its economy from being a recipient of innovation to producing it. One way of achieving this, as the experiences of the Asian Tigers (Hong Kong SAR, China; Singapore; Republic of Korea, and Taiwan, China) have shown, is to maintain FDI and export-oriented policies—as Costa Rica has successfully done over the last three decades—while at the same time strengthening the ability of the country to innovate through increased investment in education and infrastructure and through greater exposure to advanced technologies.

This chapter is organized as follows. The next section provides a summary of Costa Rica's experience with FTAs and the potential impact of CAFTA-DR on FDI and exports in the high-tech sector. Then the chapter analyzes the trends in FDI and exports in the high-tech sector of Costa Rica before and after CAFTA-DR, using secondary sources. Thereafter, the perspective of MNCs on CAFTA-DR's effects on their performance is presented, drawing on an online survey of high-tech firms in the FTZs. Last, the chapter analyzes the effect of CAFTA-DR at the firm level based on interviews conducted with a selected sample of firms.

The Impacts of FTAs on FDI and Exports in Costa Rica's High-Tech Sector

Costa Rica launched a trade liberalization-based development strategy in the mid-1980s. The country unilaterally reduced the average import tariff from 46.3 percent in 1982 to 16.8 percent in 1989 (Monge-Ariño 2011). The establishment of FTZs in 1981 and tax incentives to attract FDI rapidly transformed Costa Rica into a high-tech manufacturing exporter (Trejos 2008). Intel's decision to open an assembly and test plant in Costa Rica in 1997 paved the way for many other high-tech companies to invest in the country, with FDI in targeted knowledge-based sectors reaching 65 percent in the following 15 years (Rodríguez-Clare 2001; OECD 2012). Around the same time, the country signed trade agreements with Mexico in 1995, Canada, Chile, and the Dominican Republic in 2002, states of the Caribbean Community (Barbados, Guyana, and Trinidad and Tobago) between 2005 and 2006, and Panama in 2008 (Monge-Ariño 2011). These agreements helped Costa Rica diversify exports and increase the share of manufactured products in total exports, reducing dependence on primary products (Ferreira and Harrison 2012).

With CAFTA-DR, Costa Rica carried out changes to its legal framework, consolidating further gains from trade. Costa Rica signed the CAFTA-DR trade agreement in 2004, and it ratified the agreement in January 2009, at which point it came into effect. The United States has traditionally been Costa Rica's largest trade partner, with 45 percent of Costa Rican exports going to the United States and 45 percent of imports coming from the United States. Only 16 percent of its exports went to Central America and only 5 percent of its imports came from other CAFTA-DR members before the agreement was implemented (Hicks, Milner, and Tingley 2014). Besides eliminating tariffs and reducing non-tariff bar-riers between member countries, CAFTA-DR also introduced changes to the legal framework of member countries, ensuring a secure and predictable environ-ment for investors, with a commitment to develop an appellate mechanism for investor-state disputes (Frutos, Teekasap, and Samii 2011). These modifications increased the attractiveness of member countries to foreign investors. The agree-ment provides protection for all forms of investment, including enterprises, debt, concessions, contracts, and intellectual property (Francois, Rivera, and Rojas-Romagosa 2007). Chapter 14 of e-commerce in CAFTA-DR introduces the digi-tal product concept and blocks possible future tariffs on these products (Villalobos and Monge-Gonzalez 2011). CAFTA-DR also meets the labor objec-tives set out by the U.S. Congress and grants workers improved access to proce-dures that protect their rights (Francois, Rivera, and Rojas-Romagosa 2007).

Several studies have looked into the potential impact of CAFTA-DR on FDI inflows. Frutos, Teekasap, and Samii (2011) find that CAFTA-DR will positively affect FDI inflows in Costa Rica by lowering export tariffs and providing protec-tions for investors. They conclude that as a result of continuing FDI inflows the manufacturing sector will develop further. In another study, Francois, Rivera, and Rojas-Romagosa (2007) demonstrate that the increase in FDI and capital stock would be the biggest welfare improving mechanism of CAFTA-DR. However, they also point out that an increase in FDI inflows does not necessarily foster economic development without positive knowledge spillovers.

CAFTA-DR is also expected to diversify Costa Rican exports' incorporation in GVCs through FDI. Costa Rica contributes to at least five major high-tech GVCs: electronics, medical devices, automotive, aeronautic/aerospace, and film/broadcasting devices (Monge-Ariño 2011). These GVCs benefit from economies of agglomeration, attracting more investment from other firms and thus further strengthening Costa Rica's place in GVCs. Twenty-four firms are primarily engaged in the electronics industry, of which only six are producing final products (Gereffi et al. 2013).[1] The medical devices industry consists mostly of U.S. firms, with most significant growth occurring after the implementation of CAFTA-DR, and growth in the sector has been driven by export-oriented strategies.[2] The nascent aerospace industry in Costa Rica—with no lead firms, a relatively small labor force, and limited access to finance and technological expertise—struggles to expand (Gereffi et al. 2013).

Even if CAFTA-DR has a significant positive effect on both the FDI inflows and high-tech exports—as one might assume—this does not automatically translate into long-term growth. Ferreira and Harrison (2012) challenge the view that government-backed export diversification based on FDI is the main driver of long-term economic growth. They show that neither vertical nor horizontal diversification is associated with economic growth in Costa Rica. The main challenge to development is not only to increase FDI and trade volume but also to ensure backward links from knowledge-based industries to the local economy to generate positive spillovers and enter a virtuous circle (Giuliani 2008).

CAFTA-DR and FDI in the High-Tech Sector: Evidence from Secondary Data

An analysis of the links between CAFTA-DR and FDI inflows should consider the key developments related to the high-tech sector. First, Costa Rica's promotion of its high-tech sector started in 1981 with the passage of a law creating FTZs. This law was passed to promote the export of nontraditional products and attract FDI (Monge-Gonzales, Rosales-Tijerino, and Arce-Alpízar 2005). The second key turning point for Costa Rica's high-tech sector was when Intel moved part of its production to Costa Rica in 1997.[3] Intel played a vital role in the development of the sector through three channels: (a) it had a direct impact on employment, investment, trade, output, and the development of technology cluster; (b) it served as a catalyst for repositioning Costa Rica as an attractive investment location, through its impact on the country's technical education, incentives laws and regulations, and infrastructure (MIGA 2006); and (c) it increased the confidence of foreign investors through the demonstration effect. Third, the recent global financial crisis coinciding with the passage of CAFTA-DR also impacted the sector.

FDI inflows increased remarkably to member countries after signing in 2004, apart from a temporary downturn coinciding with the global financial crisis (see figure 2.1). FDI flows from the United States, Latin America, and Europe surged throughout the two periods of CAFTA-DR (2004–2008 and 2009 onward) while in the case of Mexico there was a marked increase after CAFTA-DR came into effect in 2009 (see figure 2.2). The increase in Mexico's FDI after CAFTA-DR was a result of the investment of América Móvil (Claro) that started operating in Costa Rica in 2011 after the liberalization of the telecommunications industry with CAFTA-DR, according to the Costa Rica Investment Promotion Agency (*Coalición Costarricense de Iniciativas de Desarrollo* [CINDE]).

Figure 2.1 Net FDI Inflows, 2000–11

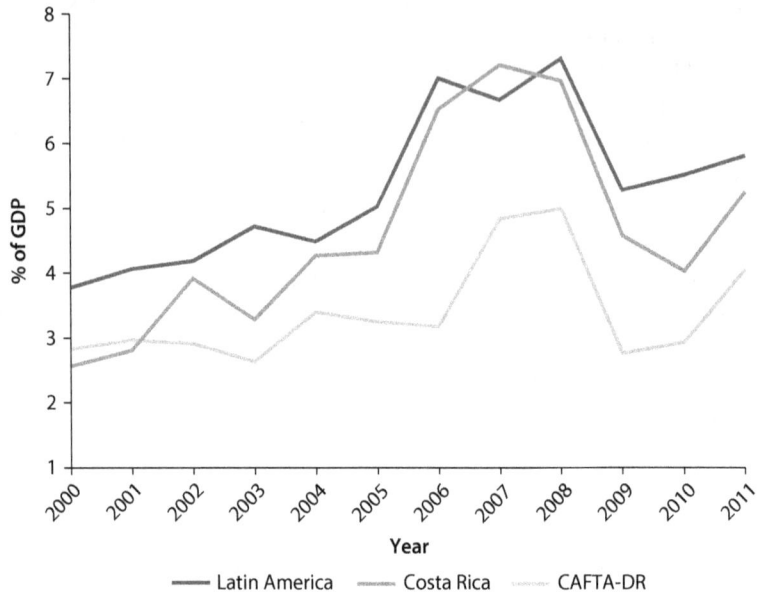

Source: Based on data from World Development Indicators.
Note: FDI = foreign direct investment.

Figure 2.2 FDI Inflows by Country of Origin

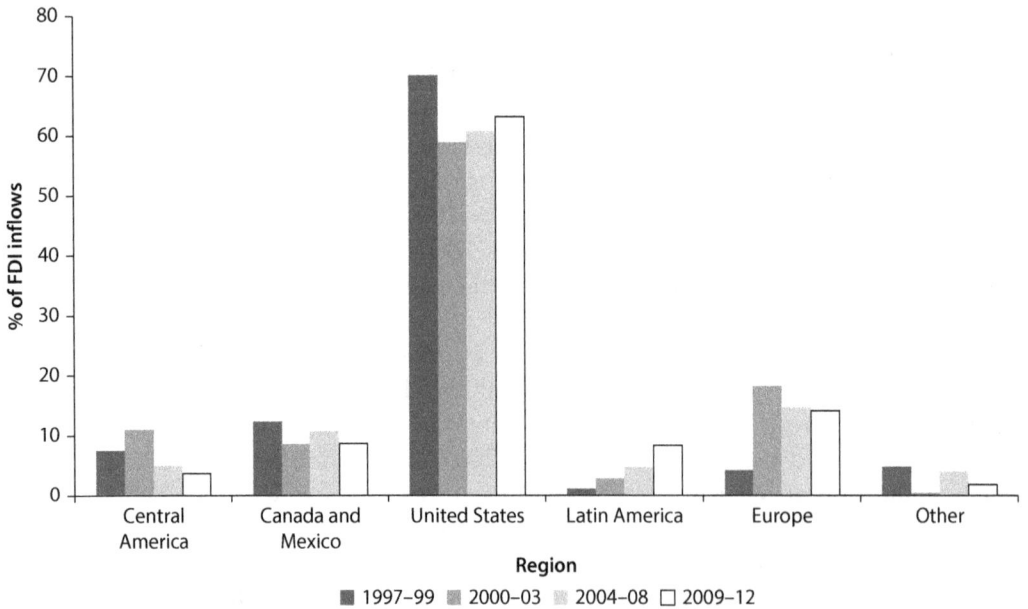

Source: Based on data from Costa Rica Investment Promotion Agency (*Coalición Costarricense de Iniciativas de Desarrollo* [CINDE]).
Note: FDI = foreign direct investment.

Costa Rica Five Years after CAFTA-DR • http://dx.doi.org/10.1596/978-1-4648-0568-4

Increased FDI inflows from Latin America after 2009 was entirely a result of the investments of Colombian companies—Nutresa, Grupo Aval, and Banco Davivienda—in Costa Rica. The increases in FDI flows from Europe during 2004–08 was due to a large Belgian investment, and the increases after 2009 were a result of the investment by the Spanish telecommunications company Telefónica in 2011 and Italian power company En el S p.A in 2012.

The distribution of MNCs across high-tech industries also changed during the last decades (see figure 2.3). Throughout the 1980s only six MNCs operated in the high-tech sector, but following the arrival of Intel in 1997 the number of MNCs increased to 18. Starting from 1999, the numbers of MNCs stagnated in electronics, while the number in medical devices and business services doubled between 2004 and 2008, and continued to increase after 2009 when CAFTA-DR came into effect. As of August 2013, 34 MNCs are present in the electronics sector, 54 in the medical device sector, and 121 in business services.

Trends in FDI flows also show a shift toward medical devices and business services and a decrease in electronics after the signing of CAFTA-DR. The average share of FDI allocated to the medical devices sector increased to 17.1 percent of net FDI flows during 2009–12, from 12.3 percent in 2000–02 (see figure 2.4). During the same period the share of electronics as a percentage of FDI flows decreased from 15.9 percent to 8.3 percent (figure 2.4). The largest growth in FDI flows to the medical device industry took place right after the implementation of CAFTA-DR, due to protections for the U.S. companies that dominate the industry.[4] The increase in FDI inflows to the business services industry, including the IT-enabled sector, after 2009 can partly be explained by the liberalization of the telecommunications sector due to CAFTA-DR. Most of the foreign investment in the business services sector after 2009 was made by U.S. companies in

Figure 2.3 Number of MNCs in High-Tech Sectors

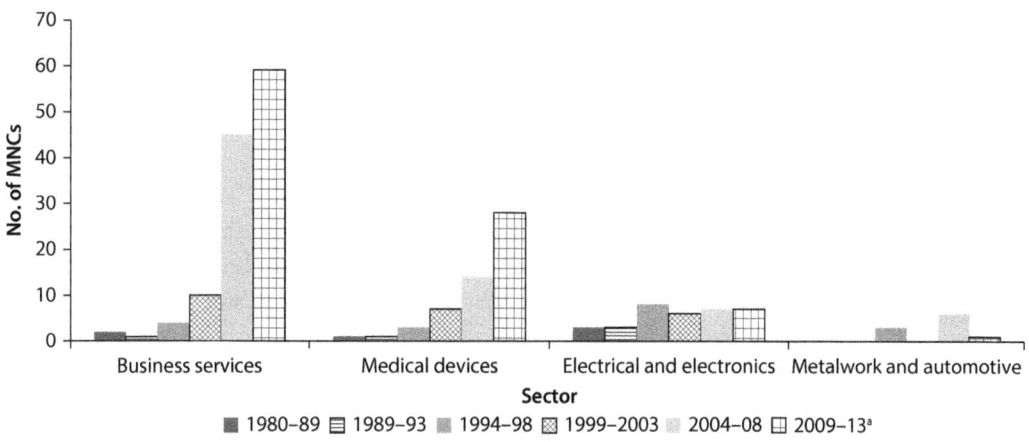

Legend: ■ 1980–89 ▤ 1989–93 ■ 1994–98 ▨ 1999–2003 ░ 2004–08 ⊞ 2009–13[a]

Source: Costa Rica Investment Promotion Agency (*Coalición Costarricense de Iniciativas de Desarrollo* [CINDE]), (official presentation's clusters), August 2013.
Note: MNCs = multinational companies.
a. Data until August 2013.

Figure 2.4 Average FDI Inflows in High-Tech Sector

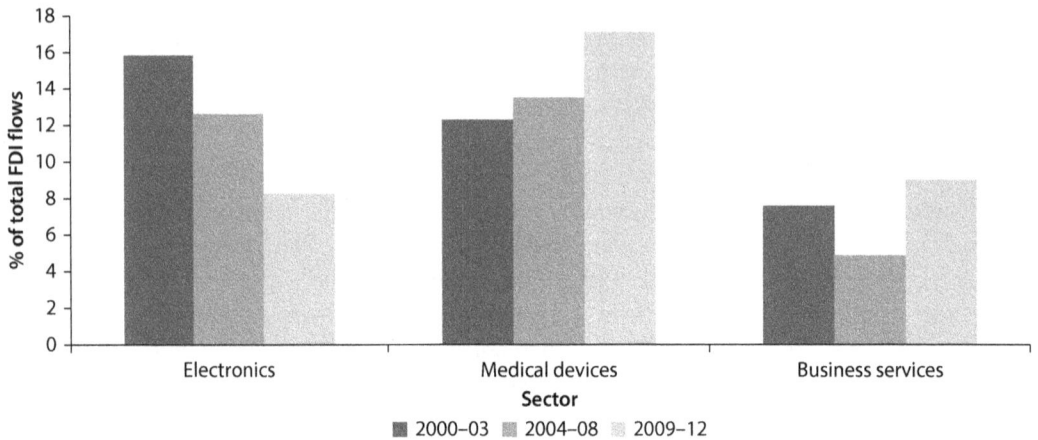

Source: Based on data from the Central Bank of Costa Rica (BCCR).
Note: FDI = foreign direct investment.

shared services, including P&G, HP, IBM, Sykes, and Wal-Mart. In sum, these trends suggest that CAFTA-DR had a direct impact on FDI inflows to the medical device and business services industries.

CAFTA-DR and Exports in the High-Tech Sector: Evidence from Secondary Data

The main goal of the FDI- and export-led development model of the government of Costa Rica has been to diversify exports away from traditional products to high-value added manufacturing products. Successful implementation of these policies, together with the educated labor force, political stability, and pro-investment public policies, enabled the country to become an important manufacturing and business service location for MNCs and transformed the country's export composition. The share of manufacturing goods exports as a share of total exports increased substantially during 1992–2000, due mainly to the exports of the MNCs in the FTZs.

This section analyzes these anticipated impacts of CAFTA-DR using secondary data from World Development Indicators (WDI), the CINDE, and the Central Bank of Costa Rica (BCCR). Given the close links of the high-tech sector of Costa Rica to MNCs, the majority of which are from the United States, CAFTA-DR is expected to contribute significantly to the exports by attracting new MNCs and expanding the investment of the existing MNCs. In addition, by strengthening intellectual property rights and the legal framework protecting foreign investors, CAFTA-DR is expected to increase FDI at the higher end of the manufacturing sector, which is more technology-intensive.

Import and export shares of national GDP increased significantly up until the onset of the global financial crisis in 2008. The first peak in both series

Figure 2.5 Costa Rica's Exports and Imports of Goods and Services, 1990–2011

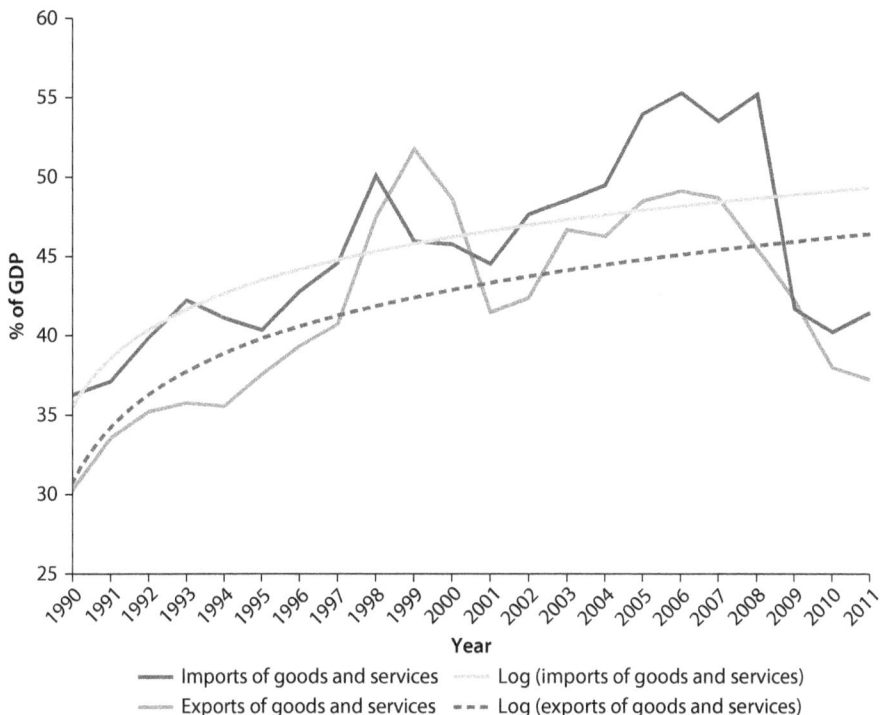

Imports of goods and services · · · · · · Log (imports of goods and services)
Exports of goods and services − − − Log (exports of goods and services)

Source: Based on data from World Development Indicators.

is observed in 1999 after the arrival of Intel, and the second one in 2006, two years after CAFTA-DR was signed (see figure 2.5). The losses due to the financial crisis were so severe that in 2010 both export and import shares of GDP dropped to their lowest levels since 1990, before starting to improve slowly in 2011.

Although FTZ exports steadily rose in absolute terms, their share of total exports fluctuated annually around 53 percent. The export levels of FTZs increased following both the signing and the entry into force of CAFTA-DR in 2004 and 2009, respectively (see figure 2.6). Although the export share of FTZs also increased after the signing of CAFTA-DR, there was no increase following its entry into force, most likely due to the interference of the global financial crisis.

Total export shares of the high-tech and low-tech sectors show diverging trends. As expected, the export share held by the low-tech sector has declined gradually since 2004, while the export share of the high-tech sector increased from 37 percent in 2004 to 47 percent in 2007 and stayed stable until the global financial crisis (see figure 2.7).

According to industry-level data from CINDE, textile exports of Costa Rica to the United States declined steadily over the course of the 2000s.

Figure 2.6 Exports of Costa Rica's FTZs, 2002–12

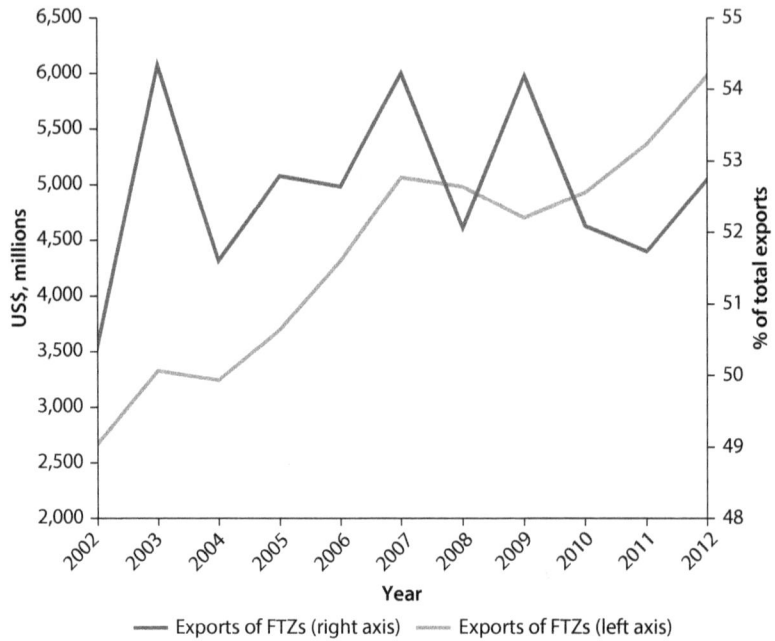

Sources: Based on data from Costa Rica Investment Promotion Agency (*Coalición Costarricense de Iniciativas de Desarrollo* [CINDE]), using data from the Center for Promotion of Foreign Trade (*Promotora del Comercio Exterior* [PROCOMER]).
Note: FTZs = free trade zones.

Figure 2.7 Exports of High-Tech and Low-Tech Sectors of Costa Rica, 2004–12

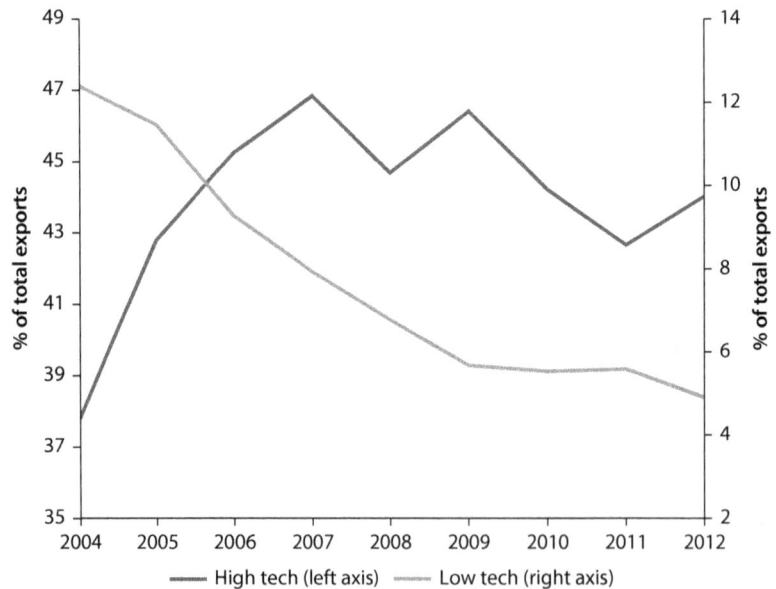

Source: Based on data from Central Bank of Costa Rica (BCCR).

Figure 2.8 Exports of Costa Rica to the United States by Sector, 2002–12

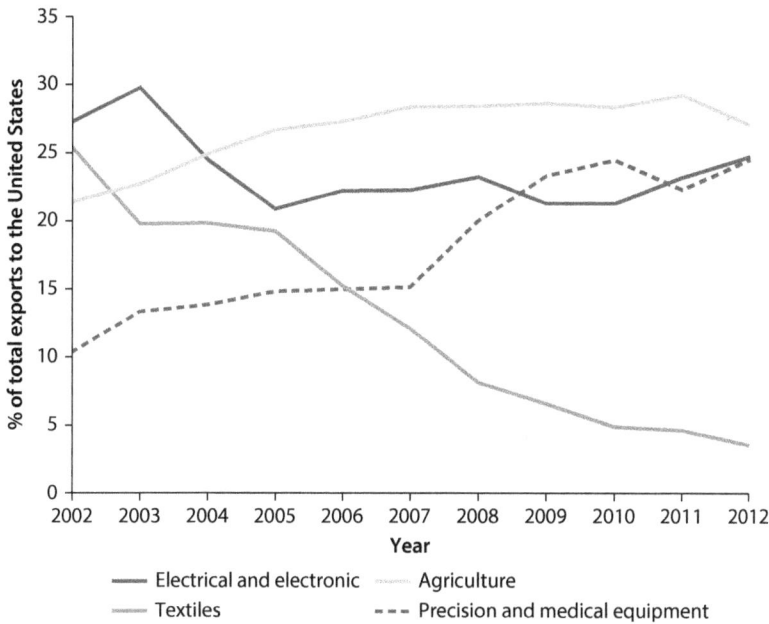

Source: Based on data from the Costa Rica Investment Promotion Agency (*Coalición Costarricense de Iniciativas de Desarrollo* [CINDE]).

The sharpest decline occurred during 2005–08, from 7.7 percent to 2.8 percent (see figure 2.8). Agricultural exports have remained stable at around 25 percent, owing to the country's internationally renowned agricultural products, innovative diversification of the sector, and the exception of some products from liberalization.

Medical instrument exports to the United States surged during 2007–12, increasing from 15 percent to nearly 25 percent (figure 2.8). In contrast, the electronics sector export share to the United States declined sharply from 2003 to 2005, falling from 30 percent to nearly 20 percent, after which it remained stable at around 22 percent. These figures exhibit similar patterns to FDI inflows to the medical instruments and electronics industries, indicating, as expected, close links between FDI and exports of high-tech industry.

As indicated above, information and communication technology (ICT) services have become one of the dominant high-tech sectors in Costa Rica during the last decade. Export shares increased impressively from about 12 percent in 2005 to about 32 percent in 2011, with a large percentage of this increase taking place after CAFTA-DR's entry into force in 2009 (see figure 2.9). Most of these changes were due to the liberalization of the telecommunications sector, which decreased the price of telecommunications, including broadband, and increased its quality substantially.

Figure 2.9 High-Tech Sector Exports in Costa Rica, 2000–11

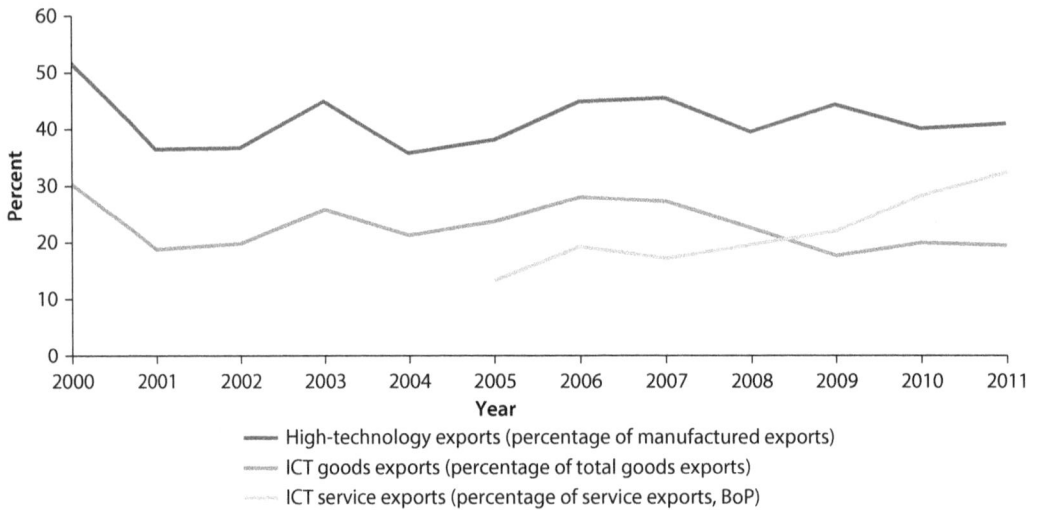

Source: Based on data from World Development Indicators.
Note: BoP = balance of payments; ICT = information and communication technology.

CAFTA-DR, FDI, and MNC Performance in the High-Tech Sector: Findings from Online Surveys

This section provides some insights on the impact of CAFTA-DR on FDI inflows to high-tech firms located in the FTZs. Using a survey of 61 firms in the software, business services, and high-tech manufacturing sectors (see box 2.1), we found that 28 percent of surveyed firms made their first investment after the entry into force of CAFTA-DR in 2009 and that all but two firms had made further investments after 2009 (see figure 2.10). The fact that almost a third of the total firms in the sample made their first investment after CAFTA-DR's implementation, and that almost all firms in the sample expanded their investment after CAFTA-DR, suggests that CAFTA-DR might have already had significant impact on FDI flows to the high-tech sector in Costa Rica, despite the short time since its entry into force and the global recession.

The majority of the surveyed firms listed the availability of skilled labor among their top three reasons for investing in Costa Rica, second only to the presence of FTZs. It is not surprising that skilled labor and FTZs were among the most cited reasons to invest in Costa Rica, as these factors have been widely covered in the literature as being one of the strengths of the Costa Rican economy (see figure 2.11). The third most cited reason was cost among high-tech manufacturing firms; on the other hand, firms in the business services and software industries cited location as the third most important factor. Interestingly, surveyed firms in high-tech manufacturing cited CAFTA-DR before location and institutional environment as a reason for investing in Costa Rica, while firms in business services ranked CAFTA-DR above institutions.

Box 2.1 Survey of Multinational Companies in High-Tech Sectors

To gain insight into the effects of CAFTA-DR on investments, production, exports, imports, and costs, we carried out a survey of firms in the high-tech sector. The questionnaire was distributed to 200 firms operating in the free trade zones (FTZs) in the high-tech sector and was administered online by the Costa Rica Investment Promotion Agency (*Coalición Costarricense de Iniciativas de Desarrollo* [CINDE]) during June through August 2013. Out of 200 firms contacted, only 62 (or 31 percent) responded to the questionnaire, but one firm was dropped as it was not in the high-tech sector. The response rate is similar to that of other enterprise surveys in Costa Rica. Although it is difficult to assess the representativeness of the sample, its distribution across sectors is similar to the distribution of firms and foreign direct investment (FDI) across the high-tech sector, suggesting that the firms in the sample can be, to a large extent, considered as representative of the high-tech industry.

Figure 2.10 Number of Surveyed Firms by Product Line of First Investment

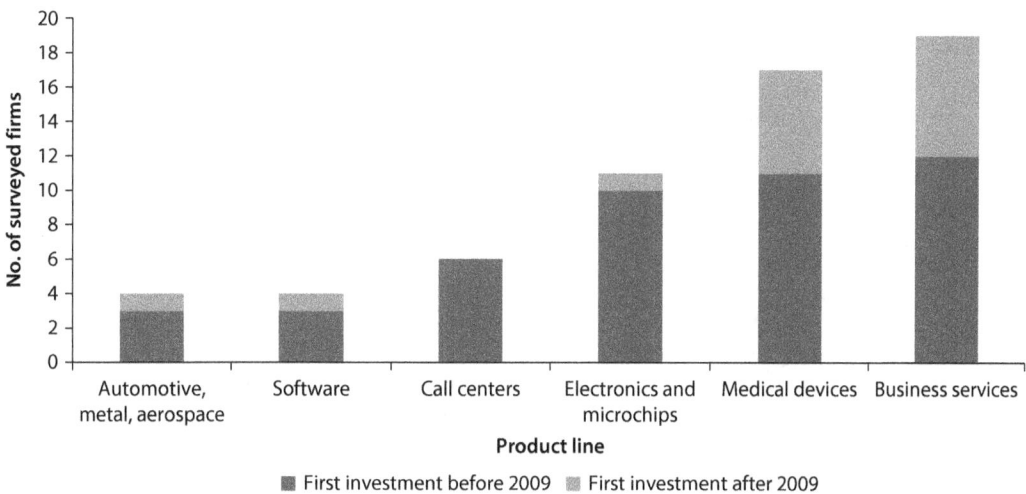

■ First investment before 2009   ▓ First investment after 2009

Source: Based on data from firm survey facilitated by the Costa Rica Investment Promotion Agency (*Coalición Costarricense de Iniciativas de Desarrollo* [CINDE]) in July–August 2013.

Although a quarter of surveyed firms indicated that CAFTA-DR did not have an effect on their operations, the rest reported positive changes in their output, investment, exports, or other economic performance indicators. About 30 percent of surveyed firms stated that CAFTA-DR increased their exports, while 28 percent indicated that it decreased their cost (see table 2.1). Only 8 percent of firms surveyed claimed that it led to increased output.

The reported effect of CAFTA-DR varied across sectors. While 43 percent of high-tech firms indicated that CAFTA-DR increased their exports (which was the most frequently chosen answer in this sector, followed by decreased cost), this was true for only 16 percent of firms in business services and 17 percent of

Figure 2.11 Top Three Reasons for Last Investment in Costa Rica by Product Line of Last Investment

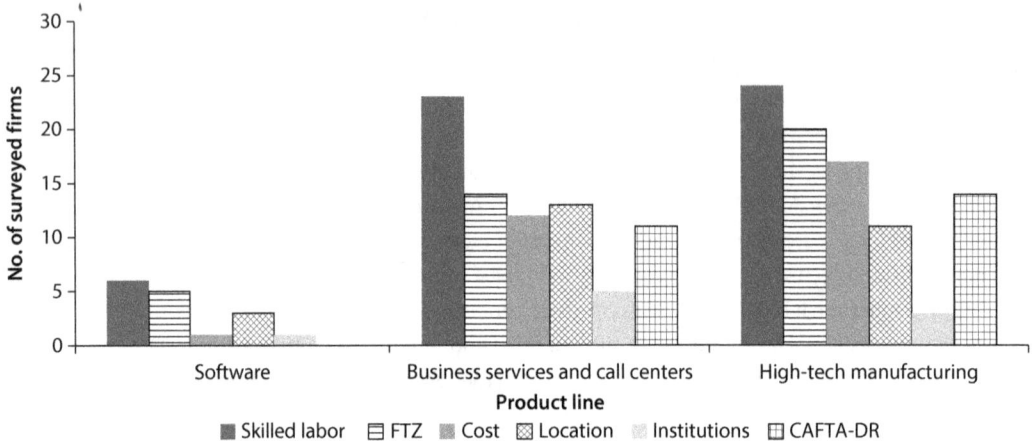

Source: Based on data from firm survey facilitated by the Costa Rica Investment Promotion Agency (*Coalición Costarricense de Iniciativas de Desarrollo* [CINDE]), July–August 2013.
Note: The product line of last and first investment is different for two firms, which explains why there are six software firms instead of four as in figure 2.10. FTZ = free trade zone.

Table 2.1 Responses: How CAFTA-DR Impacted Firm Performance, Percentage of Surveyed Firms

Product line of last investment	No. of firms	No effect	Decreased cost	Increased output	Increased exports	Other reasons
Software	6	33.3	50.0	—	16.7	—
Business services and call centers	25	32.0	36.0	8.0	16.0	16.0
High-tech	30	20.0	16.7	10.0	43.3	16.7
Total	61	26.2	27.9	8.2	29.5	14.8

Source: Based on data from firm survey facilitated by the Costa Rica Investment Promotion Agency (*Coalición Costarricense de Iniciativas de Desarrollo* [CINDE]), July–August 2013.
Note: Multiple responses were allowed. The product line of last and first investment is different for two firms, which explains why there are six software firms instead of four as in figure 2.10. — = not available.

firms in the software industry. The majority of firms in business services and the software industry responded that it decreased their cost. About 20 percent of the high-tech manufacturing firms, 32 percent of the business services firms, and 33 percent of the software firms said that CAFTA-DR has not had an impact on their economic performance.

Other effects of CAFTA-DR reported by the surveyed firms illustrated how CAFTA-DR improved the country's investment climate. The nine firms that highlighted other effects of the treaty listed the following answers: CAFTA-DR created legal certainty; provided stability and clarity to trade relations with the United States; made Costa Rica more attractive for new customers from the

United States; created the possibility of importing raw materials from other CAFTA-DR signing countries; improved Costa Rica's business environment to stimulate tier-two suppliers to follow original equipment manufacturer (OEM); and improved Costa Rica's international reputation as having a good business climate, justifying the decision to invest in Costa Rica rather than in another country.

CAFTA-DR, FDI, and Exports in the High-Tech Sector: Findings from Structured Interviews

To get further insights about the impact of CAFTA-DR in the high-tech sector, 11 firms were interviewed in depth. Through open-ended questions, these structured interviews gathered information on whether and how CAFTA-DR impacted high-tech firms on their economic decisions, such as investment, output, exports and imports. Interviews were conducted during August–September 2013 with 11 firms: three in electronics, four in medical devices, one in software, two in the IT-enabled services industry, and one in other advanced manufacturing. The firms were selected with the help of CINDE and technical experts. The Ministry of Foreign Trade (*Ministerio de Comercio Exterior* [COMEX]) helped in securing appointments with the firms in the sample.

Most of the interviewed firms indicated that CAFTA-DR had a positive impact on their investment decisions. However, the intensity of the impact and the channels through which it took place varied considerably among sectors. In the case of electronics, while one firm indicated "no impact," for the other two the impact was considerable: one is moving several product lines from Europe to Costa Rica as a result of reduced U.S. tariffs for their products under CAFTA-DR, and the other shifted from a "trial" to a "permanent" operation as a result of the treaty. In the case of medical devices, while one firm also indicated "no impact," the other three indicated that without CAFTA-DR they would either not have an operation in Costa Rica or not have expanded their pre-CAFTA-DR levels of operation. For business services firms, the benefits are more indirect in that they are associated with the liberalization of the telecom and insurance markets, and enhanced legal security due to the treaty. In software, we found an interesting effect that may also apply to other sectors, which is that the cost of bank financing declined as a result of CAFTA-DR, albeit through indirect channels: local banks are funded by U.S. banks, and those banks estimate that Costa Rica's country risk is lower than before due to CAFTA-DR. In consequence, their loan rates for local banks have been reduced, and some of this rate reduction has been passed on to local borrowers.

Interviewed firms see CAFTA-DR as a commitment to stable trade and investment policies. All except one firm considered that CAFTA-DR provided additional legal security—clear and stable "rules of the game"—and that it signaled Costa Rica's commitment to its current trade and FDI policies. This is particularly important as the confidence of foreign firms was badly shaken when the country discussed a change in the taxation regime for companies operating in FTZs not long after the current regime had been approved by a unanimous vote in the Legislative Assembly in 2009. One firm even mentioned that CAFTA-DR provided protection against a possible return to protectionism in U.S. trade policy. CAFTA-DR was credited with bringing more legal security by providing treaty-based preferential access to the U.S. market—instead of the unilateral and hence revocable concessions under the Caribbean Basin Initiative (CBI)—and also a conflict resolution mechanism in case of disputes between foreign investors and the government of Costa Rica. For the one software firm in our sample, it provided increased legal security through a surprising channel: enforcement of intellectual property rights in Central American countries where these rights were feebly enforced, or not enforced at all, prior to CAFTA-DR.

Among some of the interviewed firms, CAFTA-DR appears to have increased product lines and local linkages. For example, three companies, one each in the electronics, medical devices, and "other manufacturing" sectors, indicated that they were bringing new product lines to Costa Rica. Only in the case of electronics, however, was this due to reduced import tariffs as a result of CAFTA-DR; in the other two cases, increased investor confidence seems to have been the key factor in the decision. One firm in the electronics sector and one in the medical devices sector indicated that, as a result of CAFTA-DR, some of their clients were either expanding or setting up operations in Costa Rica, so that their local sales were increasing. Two firms in the electronics sector indicated that they were trying to source their imports from CAFTA-DR countries, and one of them is specifically trying to strengthen its Costa Rica-based supply chain.

Seven out of 11 interviewed firms reported that rejection of CAFTA-DR could have had a negative impact on them. One firm in the electronics sector indicated it would not have set up a permanent operation in Costa Rica without CAFTA-DR. Three out of four firms in the medical devices sector and one in the services sector indicated that while they would not have shut down the operations they had at the time of rejection, they would have been unlikely to make further investments in Costa Rica. A stable, rather than growing, market was the estimated impact of the software firm, and a possible relocation outside Costa Rica of their main raw materials supplier could have been the consequence for the firm in the "other manufacture" sector.

Other impacts of CAFTA-DR include effects on competitiveness and origin of imports. Seven out of 11 firms estimated they were more competitive (or Costa Rica was more competitive as an investment destination) as a result of CAFTA-DR: one in the electronics sector; two in the medical devices sector; and all firms in the services, software, and "other manufacture" sectors. CAFTA-DR had no impact on the destination of exports, but it has had a small impact on the origin of imports. As some firms try to develop Costa Rica or CAFTA-DR-based supply chains, this impact could increase over time. All firms in the electronics, medical devices, and services sectors indicated that their sectors were growing very quickly, and agreed that CAFTA-DR was helpful in increasing such growth. Some of them even identified CAFTA-DR as the decisive growth factor.

The results of our interviews suggest that CAFTA-DR was relevant for foreign investors. For most investors CAFTA-DR has been clearly an important factor in deciding to set up or to expand operations in Costa Rica. While CAFTA-DR has not fundamentally altered the economic conditions under which these firms operate—import tariffs in Costa Rica and the United States or income taxes in Costa Rica—CAFTA-DR has made a big difference by substituting treaty-based preferential access conditions to the U.S. market for the unilateral concessions that had been granted as part of the CBI. One interviewee indicated that, as Costa Rica "graduated" from poor to middle-income status, the likelihood of keeping CBI benefits would have declined over time.

Just as important, CAFTA-DR reassured investors of the Costa Rican government's commitment to its current trade and FDI attraction policies. By providing policy continuity, clear and stable "rules of the game," and mechanisms for conflict resolution between investors and the government of Costa Rica, CAFTA-DR increased investor confidence and played a key role in the decision to set up or expand the operations of most of the firms that we interviewed.

Notes

1. In 2011, electronics exports worth US$2.14 billion represented 20.4 percent of the country's total exports. These exports are highly concentrated on one product group—electronic integrated circuits, processors, and controllers—which represents 86.9 percent of electronics exports. The top export destinations are the United States (31.9 percent); Hong Kong SAR, China (23.5 percent); and the Netherlands (19.2 percent).

2. While firms first entered Costa Rica for low-cost manufacturing, they rapidly expanded their operations and upgraded their products, with total exports amounting up to US$1.3 billion in 2011.

3. Numerous studies examined why Intel decided to invest in Costa Rica and not in other countries, including Brazil, Chile, and Mexico, and find that the location of the country, its educated labor force, and its political stability played a key role in Intel's decision. Committed efforts of the government of Costa Rica, led by the Ministry of Foreign Trade (*Ministerio de Comercio Exterior* [COMEX]) in collaboration with the Costa Rica Investment Promotion Agency (*Coalición Costarricense de Iniciativas de Desarrollo* [CINDE]), to persuade Intel of the advantages of investing in Costa Rica have been widely cited as the critical factor for Intel's decision (Larrain, López-Calva, and Rodríguez-Clare 2000).

4. According to CINDE, the largest increase in FDI inflows to the medical devices industry in 2010 was due to the investment of U.S. companies in Costa Rica, including St. Jude Medical, Sterigenics, Tegra Medical, NDC, and others.

References

Ferreira, G. F. C., and R. W. Harrison. 2012. "From Coffee Beans to Microchips: Export Diversification and Economic Growth in Costa Rica." *Journal of Agricultural and Applied Economics* 44 (4): 517–31.

Francois, J. F., L. Rivera, and H. Rojas-Romagosa. 2007. *Economic Perspectives for Central America after CAFTA-DR: A GTAP-Based Analysis.* https://www.gtap.agecon.purdue.edu/resources/download/3448.pdf.

Frutos, D., P. Teekasap, and M. Samii. 2011. "CAFTA-DR Effects on FDI Inflows, Growth, and Distribution of the Workforce in Costa Rica: A System Dynamics Approach." *The International Trade Journal* 25 (3): 372–93.

Gereffi, G., P. Bamber, S. Frederick, and K. Fernandez-Stark. 2013. "Costa Rica in Global Value Chains: An Upgrading Analysis." Center on Globalization, Governance & Competitiveness, Duke University.

Giuliani, E. 2008. "Multinational Corporations and Patterns of Local Knowledge Transfer in Costa Rican High-Tech Industries." *Development and Change* 39 (3): 385–407.

Hicks, R., H. V. Milner, and D. Tingley. 2014. "Trade Policy, Economic Interests, and Party Politics in a Developing Country: The Political Economy of CAFTA-DR." *International Studies Quarterly* 58 (1): 106–17.

Larrain, F., L. F. López-Calva, and A. Rodríguez-Clare. 2000. "Intel: A Case Study of Foreign Direct Investment in Central America." CID Working Paper 58, Center for International Development, Harvard University. http://www.hks.harvard.edu/var/ezp_site/storage/fckeditor/file/pdfs/centers-programs/centers/cid/publications/faculty/wp/058.pdf.

MIGA (Multilateral Investment Guarantee Agency). 2006. *The Impact of INTEL in Costa Rica: Nine Years after the Decision to Invest.* Investing in Development Series. Washington, DC: World Bank.

Monge-Ariño, F. 2011. "Costa Rica: Trade Opening, FDI Attraction and Global Production Sharing." WTO Staff Working Paper ERSD-2011-09. https://www.econstor.eu/dspace/bitstream/10419/57577/1/660181576.pdf.

Monge-Gonzales, R., J. Rosales-Tijerino, and G. Arce-Alpízar. 2005. *Cost-Benefit Analysis of the Free Trade Zone System: The Impact of Foreign Direct Investment in Costa Rica.* Washington, DC: Organization of American States Office of Trade, Growth and Competitiveness.

OECD (Organisation for Economic Co-operation and Development). 2012. *Attracting Knowledge-Intensive FDI to Costa Rica: Challenges and Policy Options.* Making Development Happen Series 1. Paris: OECD. http://www.oecd.org/countries/costarica/E-book%20FDI%20to%20Costa%20Rica.pdf.

Rodríguez-Clare, A. 2001. "Costa Rica's Development Strategy Based on Human Capital and Technology: How It Got There, the Impact of Intel, and Lessons for Other Countries." *Journal for People-Centered Development* 2 (2): 311–24.

Trejos, A. 2008. "Country Role Models for Development Success: The Case of Costa Rica." Helsinki. http://www.econstor.eu/handle/10419/45106.

Villalobos, V., and R. Monge-González. 2011. "Costa Rica's Efforts Toward an Innovation-Driven Economy: The Role of the ICT Sector." In *The Global Information Technology Report 2010–2011*, edited by S. Dutta and I. Mia, 119–26. Geneva, Switzerland: World Economic Forum and INSEAD.

CHAPTER 3

Insurance: The End of a Monopoly, and a New Beginning for a Market

Craig W. Thorburn

Introduction and Summary

The Dominican Republic–Central America–United States Free Trade Agreement (CAFTA-DR) imposed significant change on the insurance sector. A new insurance law was required for the liberalized market, a supervisory authority needed to be established and developed to full functionality, and the National Insurance Institute (*Instituto Nacional de Seguros* [INS]), the existing monopoly insurer, needed to adjust to the new environment. Until liberalization, the life insurance sector had been mostly nascent, while the non-life business showed a penetration[1] above regional comparators but had tended to follow international pricing cycles with some amplification.[2]

It is widely accepted that without CAFTA-DR, there would have been no liberalization in the insurance sector. The market is now functioning in a competitive and open manner. New entrants have been established and are actively competing with the INS, which is responding to the competitive landscape with its own innovations and strategies. Although CAFTA-DR was the trigger for the liberalization, it is notable that all new insurers have entered from outside the territories of the Central American signatories to the agreement.

Since liberalization, the market has shown healthy growth and improved efficiency, and provided a broader range of services to clients at better value. At the same time, analysis suggests that early progress toward the new market structure is slower than the average of other comparable countries, though progress is not significantly out of line with expectations.

This chapter makes a number of recommendations:

- The liberalization of compulsory automobile and occupational risk insurance will likely require specific attention from the Superintendency of Insurance (*Superintendencia General de Seguros* [SUGESE]), particularly regarding adequate statistics for pricing and provisioning, and arrangements for the treatment of cases involving uninsured or unidentified motorists or employers.

- The expansion by the INS into new business lines and new jurisdictions should be implemented carefully and cautiously, and can benefit from learning the lessons of other entities that have tried and failed in similar endeavors.
- Continuing to develop supervisory capacity should be an ongoing priority as SUGESE staff continues to grow into their supervisory roles.

The chapter offers a summary of the most relevant legislative changes, covers market dynamics since liberalization, and then discusses what might be concluded from comparisons with other CAFTA-DR countries and markets that have liberalized. Some conclusions and policy recommendations are included in the final section.

Legislative Change

When CAFTA-DR was signed in 2004, steps to overhaul the insurance market were set in motion. With a history dating back to the Insurance Monopoly Act of 1922, the insurance market in Costa Rica had been operated through the INS. CAFTA-DR included an important policy decision to open the market. It is widely recognized that, absent the motivation from CAFTA-DR, the insurance market was unlikely to have liberalized.

In 2008, a new insurance law provided the key mechanism for liberalization. The Insurance Law (*Ley Reguladora del Mercado de Seguros*) No. 8653 was enacted on August 7, 2008. The law abolished the INS's monopoly for most classes of insurance, albeit with a later deadline for compulsory automobile and occupational risk insurances. With limited exceptions, all insurance activity in Costa Rica has to be conducted by authorized organizations.[3] Insurers can be life, non-life, or composite. Local entities may be cooperatives or public limited companies, although state owned banks may act only as minority shareholders with the INS. Foreign insurers may operate as locally incorporated entities or branches. The main regulations were issued shortly after the law was enacted.[4] The authorities also issued a range of *acuerdos* and other circulars to clarify the requirements on insurers, intermediaries, and other relevant actors in the insurance sector.[5]

The same law established the supervisory authority (SUGESE). At first, SUGESE operated within the pension superintendence. Operational separation was established in 2010, and SUGESE now has a maximum permitted staff of 41, organized in three divisions (regulation and authorization, supervision, and legal). From the commencement of the law, it has conducted a program of active on-site inspections to supplement off-site operations and established a complaint-handling service. SUGESE has indicated that it would like to move to a more risk-based supervisory approach. SUGESE is financed by an allocation from the Central Bank of Costa Rica (BCCR), although is substantively independent of it.

Investment and solvency regulations have been designed in line with an open but prudent approach. Minimum entry requirements for capital are set at levels that do not act as a barrier to entry for serious insurers.[6] Investment requirements require an overall prudent approach. Limitations include the need for investments to be channeled into publicly offered securities in Costa Rica or similar instruments in other jurisdictions.

Most products operate under a "file-and-write" system, but active approval is required for compulsory business lines. Initially, the review was motivated to give greater weight to consumer protection, so it focused more on the products issued in volumes (by the INS). This slowed approval for some newer insurers, leading some to comment that the process was not very fast at first. All insurers could leverage existing approvals, as SUGESE intended that they provide a solid benchmark. In mid-2013, legal issues were fully determined such that private insurers could participate in occupational risk and compulsory third-party automobile insurance markets. These products have a standard benefit and coverage structure, and pricing is approved by SUGESE.[7] Although it is not clear how many of the current insurers or potential new entrants will be attracted to this business, it is likely that SUGESE will have to review the arrangements for oversight of pricing, adequate data available to the market, and the treatment of special cases, such as those involving unidentified or uninsured drivers.

The legal framework was further enhanced with the issue of an insurance contract law, the *Ley Reguladora del Contrato de Seguros*, in September 2011. SUGESE followed up the publication with regulations that support the law.[8] This law allows more flexible interventions in consumer protection and policy wording issues, so SUGESE can feel more comfortable with a more traditional file-and-write approach.[9]

The liberalization under CAFTA-DR is not a one-way street. The law also made provision for the possibility that the INS may consider operating in other markets. After some clarification of the form that such engagement should take, this path is now clear and unrestricted. The INS has applied to operate in Nicaragua and registered its trademark in a number of other countries. In the past, the INS has also written some inward reinsurance (the reinsurance or assumption of risks written by another insurer) and has several portfolios in run-off. The leading market position that the INS has in Costa Rica suggests that both geographic and product diversity expansion should be beneficial and positive. However, the experience of other insurers in similar situations is not always positive; the INS should learn from these experiences and proceed with caution.

Market Dynamics

Market premium has been growing in a healthy fashion since liberalization, particularly in the nascent life sector. By 2012, written premiums for all classes of business totaled CRC 466.16 billion (US$924 million) of which non-life premiums represented 80 percent. In local currency terms, this was an increase of slightly more than 16 percent over 2011 figures. As expected, when the market was liberalized life insurance was substantially less developed, and offered considerable potential for growth (see table 3.1).

Table 3.1 Trends in Market Size and Development

	Years					Rates of growth (percentage per year)		
	2002	2007	2010	2011	2012	1 year	5 years	10 years
Insurance premium (local currency, millions)								
Life insurance	13,726	28,646	51,152	69,192	93,050	34.5	26.6	21.1
Non-life insurance	109,407	225,028	326,599	331,999	373,105	12.4	10.6	13.1
Total	123,133	253,674	377,750	401,191	466,156	16.2	12.9	14.2
Insurance premium (US$, millions)								
Life insurance	38	55	97	137	184	34.8	27.2	17.1
Non-life insurance	305	436	621	657	740	12.6	11.1	9.3
Total	343	491	718	793	924	16.5	13.5	10.4
Insurance penetration (premium to GDP)								
Life insurance	0.23	0.21	0.27	0.33	0.41	22.9	14.3	6.1
Non-life insurance	1.81	1.65	1.73	1.60	1.64	2.7	−0.1	−0.9
Total	2.03	1.87	2.00	1.93	2.05	6.2	2.0	0.1
Insurance density (premium per capita) in local currency								
Life insurance	3,364	6,437	10,977	14,628	19,386	32.5	24.7	19.1
Non-life insurance	26,815	50,568	70,086	70,190	77,730	10.7	9.0	11.2
Total	30,180	57,005	81,062	84,818	97,116	14.5	11.2	12.4
Insurance density (premium per capita) in US$								
Life insurance	9.3	12.5	20.9	28.9	38.4	32.8	25.3	15.2
Non-life insurance	74.5	97.9	133.3	138.8	154.1	11.0	9.5	7.5
Total	83.9	110.3	154.2	167.7	192.5	14.8	11.8	8.7

Source: Based on data from Insurance Information Services (AXCO).
Note: In Costa Rica, the category of personal accident and health is considered to be life insurance.

Growth in the sector has been heavily influenced by global pricing cycles in the non-life sector. Levels of insurance penetration follow the global trend, consistent with a view that global market prices were the main driver of total premium figures and suggesting there has been no material change in insurance utilization (see figure 3.1). Before liberalization took effect, penetration levels rose, and after liberalization, trends have returned to match global prices. This would also be consistent with the relatively high need for reinsurance protection in Costa Rica (discussed below). However, these trends are also heavily influenced by the response of the INS to competitive pressures both in preparation for and after the arrival of competitors. Innovations in distribution and reach by insurers have increased insurance utilization, but an offsetting effect is evident in price reductions.

The market is now operating on an open, competitive basis. During 2009, a number of foreign insurers applied for authorization. By February 2010, four new insurers had been authorized and an insurance association (Costa Rican Association of Insurance and Reinsurance [*Asociación Costarricense de Aseguradores y Reaseguradores*, ACAR]) had been established. An association of private insurers was set up in 2011. By early 2013, further market entry, and the

Figure 3.1 Explaining Non-Life Insurance Penetration Trends

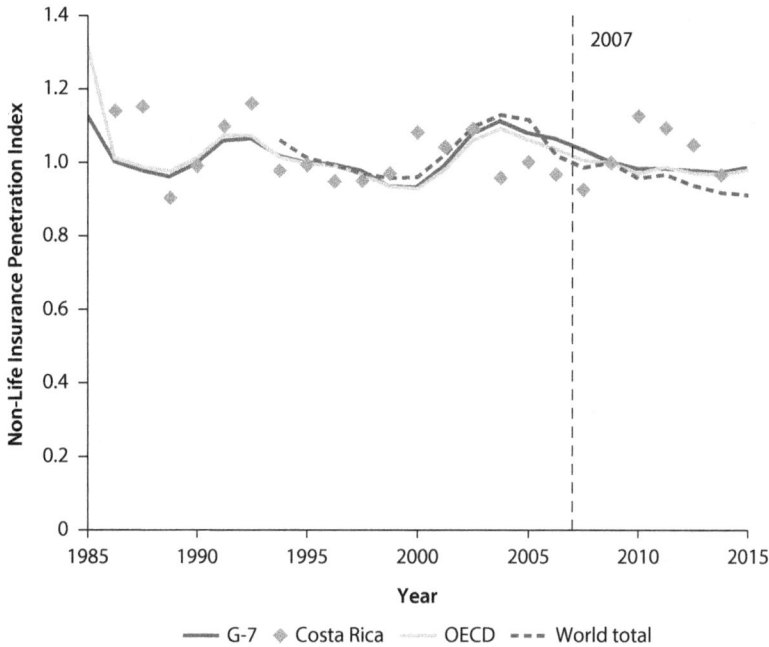

Source: Based on data from Insurance Information Services (AXCO).

Note: Comparing large aggregates in mature markets removes the impact of large volume-driven distortions, such as privatization or liberalization of particular classes, or other country-specific influences that can impact individual country statistics. With these distortions removed, the trend reflects changes in price levels rather than changes in insurance utilization (shown as solid lines on the chart). These figures, and those for Costa Rica, are then superimposed by standardizing all to 1 in 2007. As a result, the Costa Rican experience suggests higher utilization offset by price reductions beyond the effects of the global pricing cycle. G-7 = Group of Seven; OECD = Organisation for Economic Co-operation and Development.

acquisition of the Alico business by Panamerican Life, meant that 12 insurers were competing in the market (see table 3.2). None of the new entrants come from other Central American CAFTA countries, emphasizing that liberalization opened the market to all potential applicants, regardless of country of origin.

Compulsory automobile and occupational risk insurances have been liberalized after legal disputes were resolved. The opening up of the compulsory markets was supposed to occur at the start of 2011, but there was a legal dispute over whether these classes could be provided by the private insurers in the market. This was resolved in mid-2013 by the Constitutional Court, although the INS will have an ongoing advantage in these products, not least because it has extensive data on past claims. Ideally, SUGESE should review arrangements for oversight of pricing, ensuring adequate data is available to the market, and regarding the treatment of cases such as those involving unidentified or uninsured drivers.

Market composition in terms of insurers, market share, and product offerings is still developing. The market share of the INS has fallen to around 90 percent of the total market (including compulsory classes) and the Herfindahl index has reduced to 8,799 and 8,290 for life and non-life segments, respectively.

Table 3.2 Insurers Operating in Costa Rica since Liberalization

Insurer	Date of entry	Business lines	Ownership/capital	Premium in CRC millions (and market share, percent) Life	Non-life	Comments
INS	1924	Composite	Costa Rica: state owned	194,947 (93.75)	234,521 (90.82)	
Seguros del Magisterio	Feb. 2010	Life	Costa Rica: cooperative based on offering life insurance for education workers.	2,558 (1.23)	—	
Alico Costa Rica (American Life)	Feb. 2010	Life	United States	—	—	Originally part of AIG, sold to MetLife through AIG restructure. Regional business transferred to PALIC (announced November 2011, transferred November 2012).
ASSA Compañía de Seguros	Feb. 2010	Composite	Panama	887 (0.43)	14,561 (5.64)	Although registered as a composite, ASSA has only written non-life and personal accident business prior to 2012, but indicates it will enter life insurance starting in May 2013.
Mapfre	Feb. 2010	Composite	Panama/Spain	1,326 (0.64)	8,004 (3.10)	Initially registered for non-life but became composite in 2011. Re-branded from *Mundial*.
Pan American Life Insurance de Costa Rica (PALIC)	Mar. 2010	Life	United States (Louisiana)	5,006 (2.41)	—	
Aseguradora del Istmo (ADISA)	Dec. 2010	Composite	Ultimately Australian (QBE) via *QBE Del Istmo Compañía de Reaseguros, Inc.* of Panama and the *Cooperativa Nacional de Educadores*, (Coopenae) of Costa Rica	2,815 (1.35)	106 (0.04)	A life insurer, but writes some personal accident business.
Quálitas Compañía de Seguros (Costa Rica)	Jun. 2011	—	Mexico	—	1,028 (0.40)	A specialist motor insurer in Mexico.

table continues next page

Table 3.2 Insurers Operating in Costa Rica since Liberalization *(continued)*

| Insurer | Date of entry | Business lines | Ownership/capital | Premium in CRC millions (and market share, percent) | | Comments |
				Life	Non-life	
Seguros Bolivar Aseguradora Mixta	2011	Composite	Colombia	153 (0.07)	—	
Best Meridian Insurance Company	—	Life	United States (Florida)	197 (0.09)	—	
Atlantic Southern	Jul. 2012	—	United States (Puerto Rico)	47 (0.02)	—	Company also operates in the United States and British Virgin Islands as well as Puerto Rico.
Oceánica de Seguros	Jul. 2012	Composite	Venezuela, RB	—	—	
Sagicor	Feb. 2013	Composite	Barbados	—	—	

Source: Based on data from Insurance Information Services (AXCO).
Note: Premiums and market shares are shown for the most recent year (2012 or earlier) that each company participated in the market. AIG = American International Group.

The increased proportion of business represented by life insurance and the falling measure of motor insurance as a proportion of total non-life business are both indicators of a maturing market. Further, the product mix for non-life is becoming more diverse, reducing the level of risk to insurers as they hold a more diverse portfolio of risks (see table 3.3).

Legally, intermediation can be conducted through either agents or brokers, both of which can be individuals or companies. The INS had been operating through retail agents (*agencias comercializadoras*), which generated around 80 percent of business. Banks are permitted to set up insurance intermediaries and have done so particularly to deliver products packaged with lending activities.[10] SUGESE had registered 63 agency companies, 1,692 individual agents, 17 brokerage firms, and 177 individual brokers as of mid-2013. In addition there were 49 distributors of mass-marketed insurance products and two registered cross-border providers.[11] The number of registered individuals has grown steadily since liberalization, as has the diversity of distribution activities.

Innovations in distribution that are likely to increase access to insurance have been facilitated by microinsurance policies (*seguros autoexpedibles*). Products are approved for mass marketing purposes with lower and more standardized terms in some cases and include life, funeral, personal accident, and motor coverage. The INS has indicated it is distributing such products through kiosks and relationships with other distribution options such as banks, retailers, and the post office.

Despite the prohibition on placing insurance with carriers not licensed in Costa Rica, unreported informal leakage is suspected. There are no exchange control restrictions and remittances are efficiently processed by the banking sector. Visiting brokers from other markets are thought to secure some business not in compliance

Table 3.3 Competition, Development, and Performance Indicators

Competition measures	2002	2006	2007	2008	2009	2010	2011	2012
Herfindahl index								
Life insurance	10,000	10,000	10,000	10,000	10,000	9,895	8,868	8,799
Non-life insurance	10,000	10,000	10,000	10,000	10,000	9,766	8,877	8,290
Market share of largest 5 insurers (percent)								
Life insurance	100	100	100	100	100	100	99.91	99.38
Non-life insurance	100	100	100	100	100	100	100	100
Product portfolio—Product mix and diversity (percent)	2002	2006	2007	2008	2009	2010	2011	2012
Developmental indicators of products								
Life insurance to total premium	11.1	14.7	11.3	13.0	14.1	13.5	17.2	20.0
Motor insurance to total non-life insurance	45.6	43.8	44.2	42.1	40.5	38.4	37.5	39.0
Non-life product mix								
Property	23.7	17.9	20.0	18.6	22.3	20.8	19.4	18.7
Construction and engineering	2.6	3.0	3.2	—	—	—	—	—
Motor	45.6	43.8	44.2	42.1	40.5	38.4	37.5	39.0
Workers compensation	21.0	28.2	26.3	30.2	27.4	30.1	31.1	30.6
Liability	1.4	2.2	2.1	—	—	2.5	2.0	2.0
Surety, bonds, and credit	1.3	1.0	70.0	—	—	30.0	50.0	40.0
Miscellaneous	—	—	—	—	—	5.6	7.4	6.9
Marine, aviation, and transit	4.5	4.0	3.6	9.1	9.8	2.3	2.0	1.9
Personal accident and health care (non-life)	—	—	—	—	—	—	—	—
Profit and volatility (percent)	2007	2008	2009	2010	2011	2012	Average	Coeff. of variation
Claims ratios								
Property	10.60	—	—	14.34	24.81	46.14	20.24	1.113
Construction and engineering	10.22	—	—	—	—	—	22.23	1.066
Motor	39.90	—	—	47.19	53.53	52.99	57.20	0.174
Workers compensation	56.41	—	—	49.54	53.94	51.30	67.36	0.207
Liability	13.83	—	—	19.59	39.62	30.41	33.93	1.496
Surety, bonds, and credit	25.44	—	—	383.93	191.59	203.35	94.20	1.172

table continues next page

Table 3.3 Competition, Development, and Performance Indicators (continued)

Competition measures	2002	2006	2007	2008	2009	2010	2011	2012
Miscellaneous	—	—	—	34.71	17.83	25.43	25.99	0.325
Marine, aviation, and transit	24.51	—	—	34.43	50.48	48.24	34.80	0.297
Personal accident and health care (non-life)	—	—	—	—	—	—	—	—
All non-life insurance	36.24	43.09	56.57	40.25	45.73	49.24	49.60	0.161

Source: Based on data from Insurance Information Services (AXCO).
Note: — = not available.

with the insurance law, and the taxation treatment of this informal insurance is not clear, although it would appear to also avoid premium duties and fine levies.[12] A significant number of U.S. and Canadian citizens have retired to Costa Rica, and foreign non-admitted insurers are reported to target expatriates through advertising campaigns. The National Council for the Supervision of the Financial System (*Consejo Nacional de Supervisión del Sistema Financiero* [CONASSIF]) issued a regulation in late 2012 that facilitates a legal form of fronting for some commercial classes,[13] and there is no minimum retention requirement in Costa Rica.

Claims ratios reflect a profitable but not entirely stable insurance market. With the exception of the small surety portfolio, claims ratios are well below levels needed for profitable underwriting by world standards. The market claims ratio stood at just below 50 percent of premiums. The INS announced increases in compulsory third-party automobile insurance premiums in 2012 by an average of 43.25 percent after an average reduction in 2011 of 13.89 percent. Volatility measures are higher than world averages, although this may be the result of a small market, and can be expected to improve as experience develops over time.

Exposure to natural catastrophes requires careful management of risk accumulations by insurers and effective access to and use of reinsurance protection. Costa Rica is exposed to significant earthquake and active volcanic risks. Although it is not in the most active part of the hurricane region, it has been impacted by hurricanes, and tropical storms have led to significant flood events. Retention rates for the sector are heavily determined by the approach that the INS takes in the current market given its size, and there is no public information on cessions by insurer. Overall, it is reported that the market ceded around 33.8 percent of gross premiums in 2011 and 32.6 percent in 2011.

Total assets have increased in real terms, enabling the sector to play an increased role as an institutional investor. Total assets have risen as the sector grows and business becomes more mature, and that value now stands at CRC 1,484 billion. In the last two years alone, sector investments increased by 6.7 percent over and above GDP increases (see table 3.4).

The industry has become more efficient. Expense rates have declined by 10 percent over the most recent reporting periods. This can be attributed to the

Table 3.4 Total Assets (CRC Millions)

	2010	2011	2012
Assets	1,155,893	1,341,088	1,484,494
As a percentage of GDP	6.13	6.47	6.54

Source: Based on data from Insurance Information Services (AXCO).
Note: Assets are not reported separately between life and nonlife sectors.

Table 3.5 Expense Ratios (Expenses as Percentage of Premiums)

	2010	2011	2012
Administrative expenses	22.35	23.09	20.02
Acquisition costs	7.84	7.49	7.11
Total	30.19	30.59	27.13

Source: Based on data from Insurance Information Services (AXCO).
Note: Assets are not reported separately between life and non-life sectors.

impact of competitive initiatives on expense control, and to innovation from new entrants, as well as economies naturally generated from increased market size. However, to the credit of sector management, cost savings have been passed to customers (see table 3.5).

The market has overcome the initial costs of establishing operations and is now profitable. In 2010, only the INS was profitable, but the total market has reported a pretax profit of CRC 76,591 million, or 16.4 percent of gross premiums, compared to 13.6 percent of gross premiums in 2011.

At the same time, the value provided by insurance products has increased, providing a material benefit to clients as a result of competition. A 20 percent increase in claims ratios (payouts as a proportion of premiums) demonstrates increased value for money to the market and real economy. With this improved efficiency and value, a conservative estimate of the direct benefit to the real economy of the market developments since the reform is around CRC 100 billion per year so far.

Comparison with CAFTA-DR and Latin American Countries

The Costa Rican market is already substantial compared to other CAFTA-DR jurisdictions. The market is larger (in US$ premium terms) than any of the other countries and has been growing more rapidly in both life and—with the exception of measures in local currency—non-life insurances. As a result of the faster growth, the sector might be compared more appropriately to the Association of Insurance Supervisors of Latin America (*Asociación de Supervisores de Seguros de Latinoamérica* [ASSAL]) averages and ratios, suggesting a growth potential in premiums of at least 50 percent in the medium term and a life sector that is three times the current size.

The potential for continued growth and development is considerable. Costa Rica has the lowest proportion of premiums generated from life insurance of all the countries in table 3.6, highlighting that the sector has a considerable way to

Table 3.6 Comparative Insurance Market Data in CAFTA-DR and Latin America

	Costa Rica	Dominican Republic	El Salvador	Guatemala	Honduras	Nicaragua	CAFTA-DR (average)	Latin America (average)
Growth in premium in local currency (percent)								
Life	26.57	15.55	9.51	12.65	11.65	13.16	—	—
Non-life	10.64	6.97	5.10	7.46	5.41	11.84	—	—
Total	12.94	8.65	6.52	8.41	8.11	12.17	—	—
Market premium in US$ (millions)								
Life	184.44	174.16	187.43	121.60	173.50	36.62	877.75	117,289.77
Non-life	739.55	568.11	315.44	471.80	191.74	108.58	2,395.23	115,260.72
Total	924.00	742.27	502.87	593.40	365.24	145.20	3,272.98	232,549.49
Growth in premium in US$ (percent)								
Life	27.17	11.77	9.51	12.18	11.65	8.83	13.59	13.16
Non-life	11.17	3.47	5.10	7.01	5.41	7.57	6.57	10.61
Total	13.48	5.10	6.52	7.96	8.11	7.88	8.20	11.06
Insurance penetration (premium as percentage of GDP)								
Life	0.41	0.30	0.75	0.23	0.92	0.45	0.43	1.20
Non-life	1.64	0.96	1.39	0.90	1.02	1.33	1.16	1.90
Total	2.05	1.26	2.14	1.13	1.93	1.78	1.59	3.11
Growth in insurance penetration (percent)								
Life	14.26	3.94	4.88	2.99	2.58	1.19	4.98	4.20
Non-life	−0.12	−3.78	0.66	−1.75	−3.16	0.01	−1.51	1.89
Total	1.95	−2.27	2.02	−0.88	−0.68	0.30	0.00	2.29
Insurance density (premium per capita in US$)								
Life	38.43	17.95	25.66	8.04	21.16	5.28	17.25	175.52
Non-life	154.07	58.57	47.60	31.18	23.38	15.67	47.11	247.45
Total	192.50	76.52	73.26	39.22	44.54	20.95	64.36	422.97
Growth in insurance density (percent)								
Life	25.26	11.37	9.05	9.43	8.67	4.14	11.33	11.73
Non-life	9.50	3.10	4.66	4.38	2.59	2.93	4.45	9.22
Total	11.77	4.73	6.07	5.31	5.22	3.23	6.05	9.66
Herfindahl index								
Life	8,799	1,674	960	1,103	1,471	2,563	2,762	2,182
Non-life	8,290	1,507	961	1,581	1,703	2,215	2,710	1,826
Development indicators (percent)								
Life to total premium	20.0	23.5	35.0	20.5	47.5	25.2	26.8	50.4
Motor to non-life premium	39.0	38.8	19.3	28.7	33.0	46.7	34.3	35.0

table continues next page

Table 3.6 Comparative Insurance Market Data in CAFTA-DR and Latin America *(continued)*

	Costa Rica	Dominican Republic	El Salvador	Guatemala	Honduras	Nicaragua	CAFTA-DR (average)	Latin America (average)
Product mix (percentage of total non-life premium)								
Property	18.7	43.8	30.2	25.6	46.1	36.9	33.6	24.6
Construction and engineering	0.0	0.0	—	3.7	6.9	4.5	3.0	5.1
Motor	39.0	38.8	19.3	28.7	33.0	46.7	34.3	35.0
Occupational risk	30.6	—	—	—	—	—	30.6	19.6
Liability	2.6	0.0	0.0	2.1	3.0	2.4	1.7	3.7
Surety, bonds, and credit	0.4	3.7	3.5	4.9	3.3	4.6	3.4	5.0
Miscellaneous	6.9	8.7	25.4	1.6	1.7	1.2	7.6	7.8
Marine, aviation, and transit	1.9	5.0	0.0	6.8	6.0	3.7	3.9	5.3
Personal accident and health care (non-life)	—	—	21.5	26.6	—	—	24.1	19.4
Claims ratio experience								
Non-life data set average	49.60	55.83	33.63	63.29	63.13	33.75	50.03	54.70
Coefficient of variation	0.161	0.949	1.206	0.249	1.339	0.163	0.665	0.404

Source: Based on data from Insurance Information Services (AXCO).
Note: All growth rates cover the latest five years available to 2012 and are expressed in percentages per annum. CAFTA-DR averages are the average proportion of the product line; as this applies only to countries that have such a line reported in the data set, this does not add up to 100 percent. Latin American average corresponds to Association of Insurance Supervisors of Latin America (*Asociación de Supervisores de Seguros de Latinoamérica* [ASSAL]). — = not available.

go to reach the point of comparison with its neighbors, let alone broader averages. Motor insurance as a proportion of total non-life premium is higher than other countries in the CAFTA-DR group with the exception of Nicaragua, indicating scope for further maturing and diversification in the non-life sector. Diversification measures also suggest that there is room for further innovation in products to meet market opportunities. Other markets tend to have higher and more volatile claims experience with the exception of Nicaragua. The lower volatility and greater fundamental profitability inherent in the Costa Rican non-life market also suggests that the market is attractive.

Interpreting Recent Developments

The experience of other liberalizing countries can provide some clues to where the Costa Rican insurance sector may be headed. Several comparisons have been developed based on measures of market development and market shares, comparing them to markets that have similarly opened up their market from a mandated monopoly. Opening values are standardized where needed, to ensure a meaningful comparison with the Costa Rican starting position. Charts show a range of countries to highlight the range of potential outcomes and consistency of tendencies across the data set. Separately, the position of Costa Rica against the average of all countries in the comparative group is shown for clarity (see figure 3.2).

Like many countries, Costa Rica has seen progressive liberalization of product lines, and has historically had a relatively weak life sector.

Figure 3.2 Insurance Penetration Following Liberalization
premium as percentage of GDP

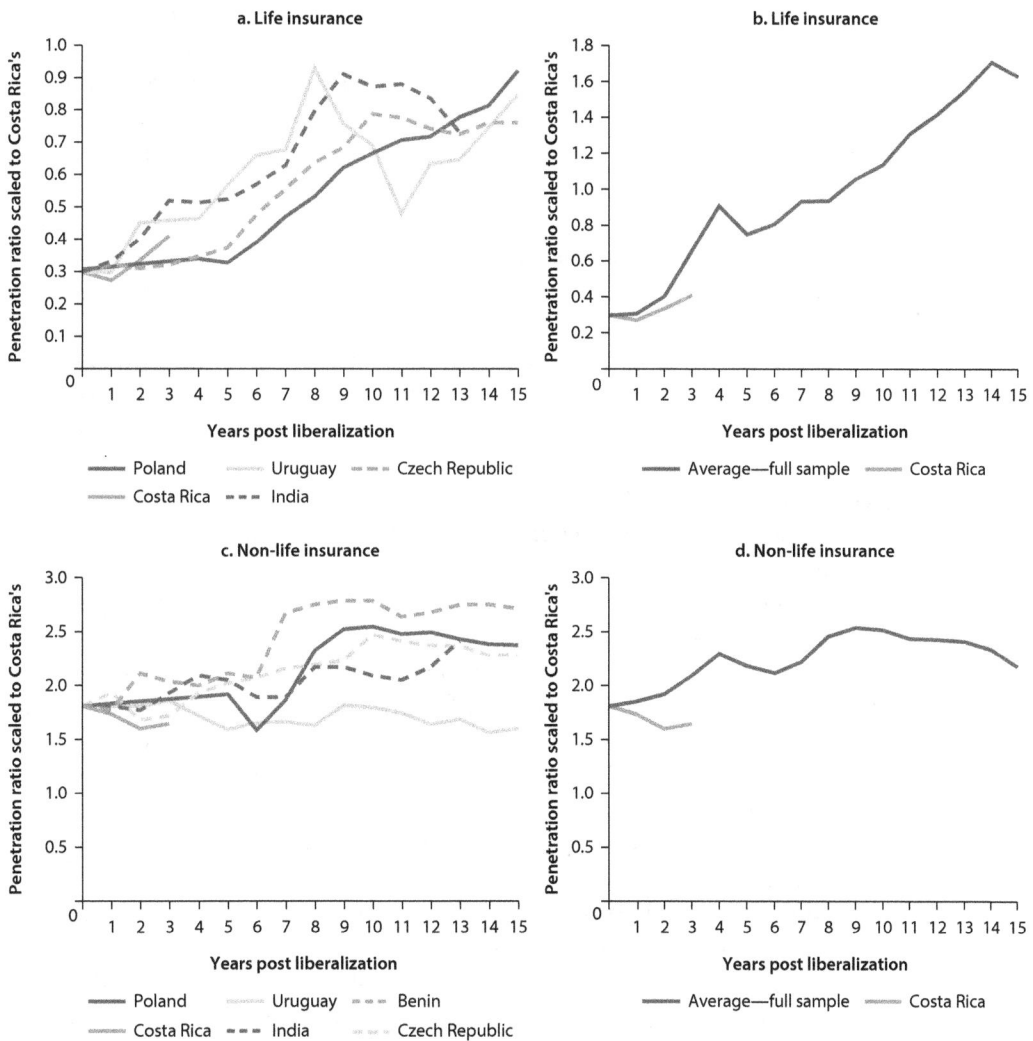

Source: Based on data from Insurance Information Services (AXCO).

Note: Penetration ratios (premium as percentage of GDP) were scaled to Costa Rica's figures. The full sample includes the following countries: Albania, Benin, Costa Rica, the Czech Republic, Ethiopia, India, Poland, and Uruguay.

Costa Rica Five Years after CAFTA-DR • http://dx.doi.org/10.1596/978-1-4648-0568-4

Costa Rica's market has seen life insurance penetration increase already, but the experience of other countries suggests there could be a considerable path of real growth ahead. If Costa Rica continues on a similar path, then the life sector can be expected to continue growth above the rate of GDP for an extended period and become very materially larger in real terms; the trends suggest that the sector could grow from 0.3 percent of GDP to four times that size in 15 years. Non-life products tend to follow GDP more closely, given the need to insure fundamental economic activities in the jurisdiction.

As would be expected, the INS has attempted to defend its market position, while new entrants focus on innovation in products and services to attract customers and explore new market segments. Sensible strategic directions at liberalization would indicate that the INS should seek to maintain market momentum in key products rather than develop new initiatives where it had limited experience. At the same time, it needed to enhance operating and administrative processes and realign business priorities.[14] New players would have been attracted to the nascent life sector where the INS had demonstrated weaker capacity, and foreign players would seek to leverage their technical experience in innovative products and distribution. Even though the market share of the INS would be expected to decrease, the increased size of the total market would in turn help the INS so long as it was able to grow its absolute premium levels and cover its fixed cost structure.

All of these trends appeared as expected after liberalization. The INS market share has fallen to around 90 percent. Premium growth in the market has meant that the INS premium has increased at 6.3 percent per annum over the last four years, and stands at CRC 429 billion in 2012. New players have been more aggressive in the life sector.

Comparisons with other countries suggest that many indicators in Costa Rica are evolving at a similar rate (see figure 3.3). The falling market share of the INS is largely in line with the experiences of other countries, and can be expected to continue for a good number of years.

The INS share of the life insurance market has held up slightly better than would be expected. One explanation for this could be the invigoration of the general concept of life insurance. Another could be the aggressive efforts of the INS to engage with distribution networks (both traditional and innovative). Also, new entrants into Costa Rica may be less innovative, as they are not, by global measures, large insurers. As a result, new entrants may not be competing as effectively as their peers in other markets.

Costa Rica's liberalization and trends are very much in line with what would be expected given the experience of other countries. New entrants are seeking to compete and innovate, and the incumbent is seeking to defend market share and meet new challenges. Costa Rica's experience, and its rate of change, is in line with other countries (see box 3.1). However, on each measure, Costa Rica's values suggest that its experience has been slightly conservative, indicating the potential for a somewhat quicker pace of change. Either way, the country's indicators and trends thus far point to continued reductions in INS market share, and sector growth and development.

Outlook

The insurance sector is already showing benefits through improved operating performance, growth, product innovation, and efficiency and is contributing more to the real economy. The more diverse product range, which is more

Figure 3.3 Pace and Direction of Liberalization on Market Shares: Costa Rica Follows a Well-Worn Path

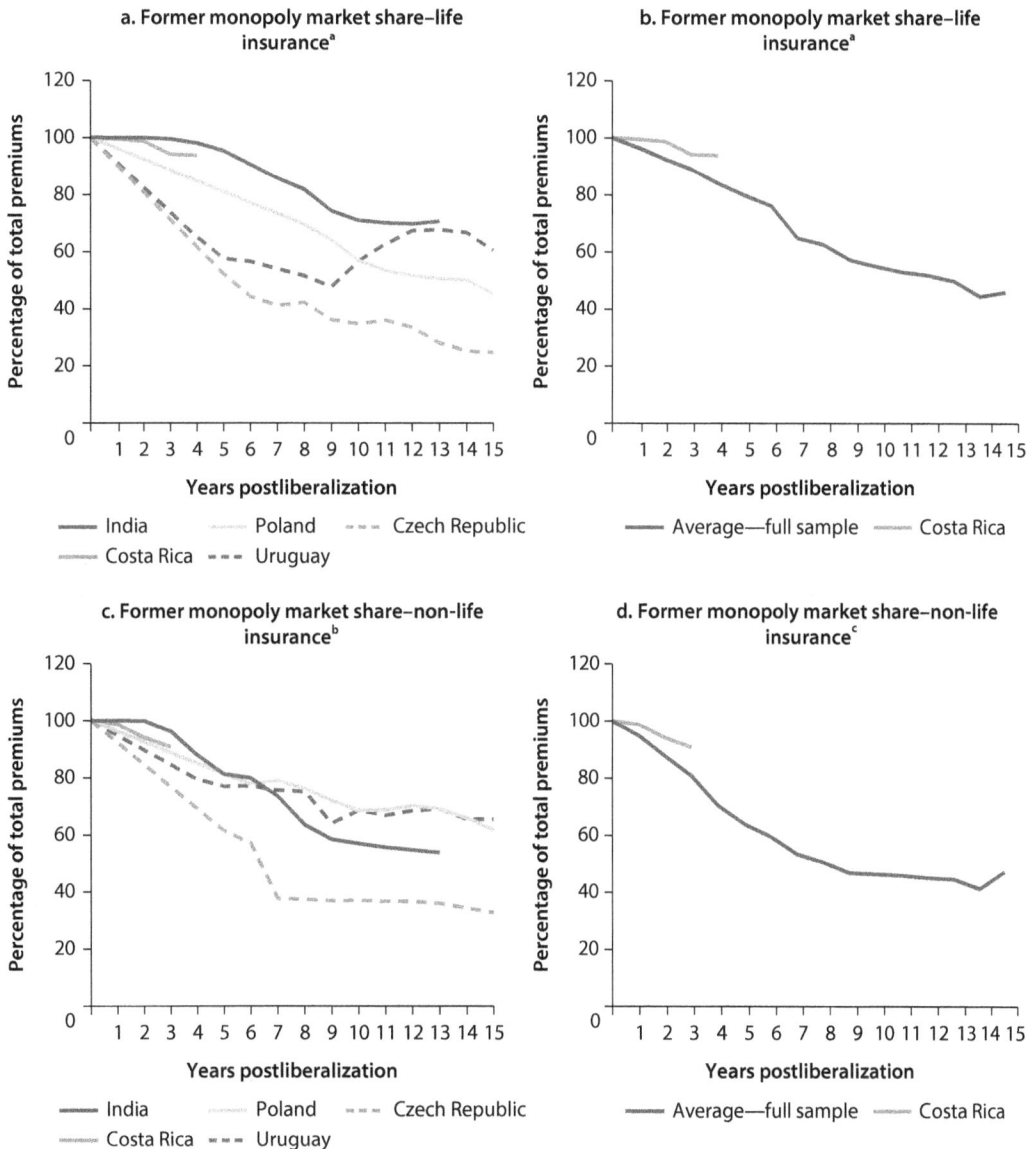

Costa Rica Five Years after CAFTA-DR • http://dx.doi.org/10.1596/978-1-4648-0568-4

Figure 3.3 Pace and Direction of Liberalization on Market Shares: Costa Rica Follows a Well-Worn Path *(continued)*

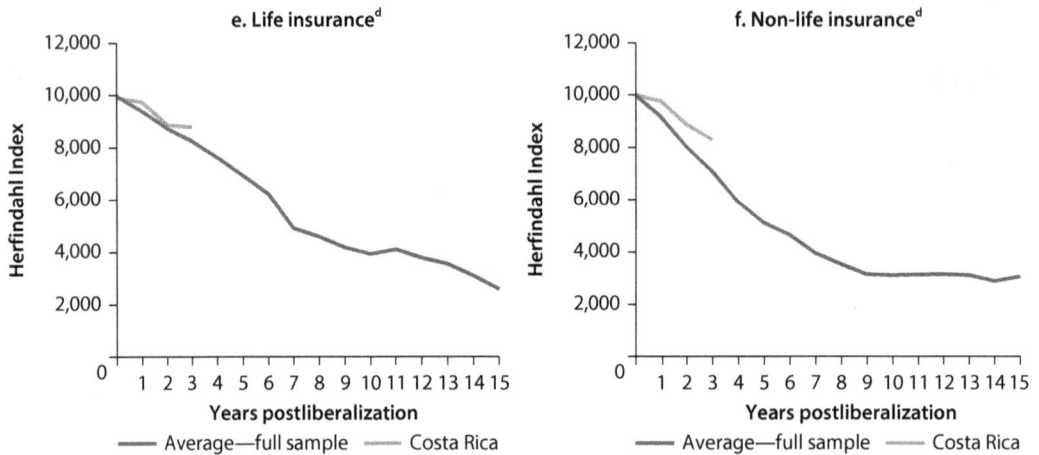

e. Life insurance[d]

f. Non-life insurance[d]

Source: Based on data from Insurance Information Services (AXCO).

Note: The full sample includes the following countries: Albania, Benin, Costa Rica, the Czech Republic, Ethiopia, India, Poland, and Uruguay.

a. The former monopoly insurer, naturally, sees a reduction in market share. Premium levels for the former monopoly insurer grew strongly despite the fall in share because of the overall market growth rates. The National Insurance Institute (*Instituto Nacional de Seguros* [INS]) share is consistent with the comparative experience in other markets so far.

b. The Costa Rican experience is similar to that of other countries, particularly in the larger non-life sector. The INS market share can be expected to reduce over time in a steady manner.

c. The INS has exceeded expectations in retaining market share in the non-life segment.

d. Consistent with the realignment of market shares, the Herfindahl measures are expected to fall over a period of 10–15 years before stabilizing and reaching a more mature stage.

Box 3.1 Comparing the Czech Republic, Poland, and Uruguay

Prior to the introduction of legislative reforms in 1994, the market in Uruguay operated as a monopoly through the state-owned *Banco de Seguros del Estado* (BSE). An exception was in cases where insurers and insurance had been grandfathered in from before the introduction of the monopoly, which largely applied to marine and cargo insurance. Once liberalized, worker's compensation, bonds, and health insurance for public sector employees remained in the portfolio of the BSE. Compulsory third-party automobile insurance was introduced in 2009.

Between 1948 and 1989, the Polish insurance sector operated as a monopoly controlled by the state-owned PZU (domestic business) and WARTA (reinsurance and hard currency insurances). After 1989, these two companies remained active in the liberalized market and were partially privatized in 1999.

In the Czech Republic, the Ceska Pojistovna lost its monopoly in 1989. However, it did not see a competitor formed until 1993; moreover, it did not lose its monopoly status in aviation until 1997, and retained its monopoly on motor insurance until 2000.

Since liberalization in these countries, both life and non-life sectors have grown and developed, and the fledgling life insurance sector has been more dynamic. Life insurance as a proportion of total premium has practically doubled in the last 15 years, from 12 percent to over 26 percent in Uruguay, and from 34 percent to just under 60 percent in Poland. The non-life sector has become less dependent on motor insurance over the same period, from nearly

box continues next page

Box 3.1 Comparing the Czech Republic, Poland, and Uruguay *(continued)*

Table B3.1.1 Comparative Statistics for Costa Rica, the Czech Republic, Poland, and Uruguay

	Costa Rica	Czech Republic	Poland	Uruguay
Land size (square kilometers)	51,100	78,864	312,683	176,215
Population in 2012 (millions)	4.80	10.50	38.10	3.38
GDP 2012 (US$, millions)	45,108	195,657	489,235	47,777
Insurance to GDP 2012				
Life insurance	0.41	1.88	2.30	0.57
Non-life insurance	1.64	2.13	1.60	1.59
Claims ratios				
Non-life Data Set Average	49.60	—	57.53	47.14
Most recent	49.24	—	63.74	49.39
Expense ratios—non-life				
Non-life data set average	29.30	—	33.60	43.20
Most recent	27.13	—	31.97	36.94
Market share held by life insurance	20.0%	—	58.9%	26.4%
Non-life market share of motor insurance	39.0%	—	56.8%	40.1%

Source: Based on data from Insurance Information Services (AXCO).
Note: GDP = gross domestic product.

45 percent of non-life premiums to 40 percent in Uruguay and from 71 percent to 57 percent in Poland, reflecting increased product innovation and diversification, which better meets the needs of the real economy (see table B3.1.1).

Although the former monopoly insurers' shares of the market have fallen steadily, these insurers have seen steady growth in premiums every year since liberalization. The exception has been during economic crisis events, and even during those crises premiums fell only marginally. Initially, the BSE wrote around 10 percent of total premiums as life insurance and 90 percent as non-life insurance, similar to the INS. Life insurance has now grown to over 25 percent of the BSE's gross written premiums. Over the last 15 years, life insurance premiums for the BSE grew at 17.6 percent per annum, and non-life insurance premiums grew by 9.7 percent per annum. Life insurance premiums at the two former monopoly insurers in Poland have grown by 10.1 percent per annum over the last 15 years, and total premiums grew by 6.5 percent per annum.

---

accessible and offers better value to clients, is likely helping those in the real economy to better manage risks. Products are offering a better value for money. Insurance assets are growing in size, allowing insurers to become more relevant as institutional investors.

The insurance sector should continue its path to a fully market-driven profile over time. Consistent with observed experience in other jurisdictions, the liberalization process has a long way to go. Developments so far are in line with expectations, but could be encouraged through continued efforts to ensure an appropriate environment that supports ongoing innovation and development.

As with all markets, the sector's development will be influenced by the operating environment, including the economic conditions in Costa Rica and globally, as well as the trends in global reinsurance prices. Diligent supervision, sound preconditions for market development, and targeted interventions to support these preconditions are expected to remain relevant.

Recommendations that can be drawn from this assessment are limited, as much of the future advantage can be expected to arise without government or policy interference. That said, it would be useful for policymakers to consider the following:

- The liberalization of compulsory automobile and occupational risk insurances will likely require specific attention from SUGESE, particularly regarding adequate statistics for pricing and provisioning, and arrangements for the treatment of cases involving uninsured or unidentified motorists or employers.
- The expansion by the INS into new business lines and new jurisdictions should proceed carefully and can benefit from learning the lessons of other entities that have tried and failed in similar endeavors.
- Continuing to develop supervisory capacity should be an ongoing priority as SUGESE staff continues to grow into their supervisory roles.

The initial phase of liberalization in the insurance sector has been positive, but the complete benefits of the initiative are not yet fully captured. As the process continues, the benefits of a more effective industry, able to provide for the needs of the real economy and enhance the well-being of all Costa Ricans, will be realized.

Notes

1. "Insurance penetration" is defined as premium divided by GDP.
2. The World Bank provided advice on these three issues in June 2004.
3. Article 2 of the Insurance Law. There are limited exceptions such that nonadmitted insurances are permitted on a cross-border basis with insurers in countries where there is a current trade agreement that makes provision for such cross-border transactions of insurance (Article 16 of the Insurance Law) and providers have to register with the SUGESE. To date, Costa Rica has undertaken commitments in cross-border trade of insurances services in the CAFTA-DR and the Association Agreement with the European Union.
4. *Reglamento sobre Autorizaciones, Registros y Requisitos de Funcionamiento de Entidades Supervisadas por la Superintendencia General de Seguros* and the *Reglamento sobre la Solvencia de Entidades de Seguros y Reaseguros* were both enacted September 24, 2008.
5. "Other relevant actors" includes actuaries, auditors, claims adjusters, and so on.
6. Minimum capital requirements in development units are CRC 3 million for either a life or non-life insurer and CRC 7 million for a composite. Reinsurers are required to have 10 million in development units. These amounts currently translate to around US$4.75 million, US$10.5 million, and US$15.5 million, respectively. Although these levels are the highest of all CAFTA-DR countries, they are far from high when compared to, for example, countries that are members of the Association of Insurance

Supervisors of Latin America (*Asociación de Supervisores de Seguros de Latinoamérica* [ASSAL]).

7. Article 29 (e) of the Insurance Law requires SUGESE authorization of tariffs for occupational risk and compulsory third party automobile insurance.

8. *Transitorio I de la Ley Reguladora del Contrato de Seguros* was issued in the same month as the law was enacted.

9. Previously, for most lines of insurance, SUGESE received a technical report and could comment or require modification within a statutory 30-day period only, so it had limited opportunity to act after this period (Article 29 [d] of the Insurance Law).

10. Banks have been permitted to act as intermediaries since 2001 in Costa Rica.

11. Two entities have registered to do specific business on a cross-border basis: (a) Factory Mutual Insurance Company (Rhode Island), to do certain international group insurance for international conglomerates, and (b) Caledonian Insurance Group (Washington), acting as a broker for aviation risks.

12. All non-life insurances are subject to a 13 percent sales tax. The fire brigade charge is 4 percent of premiums and is charged to all insurance classes as part of the quoted premium. It came about because the INS used to include this rate in all products and was administered by the fire brigade before liberalization. A 33 percent charge is placed on compulsory automobile insurance, although there is little practical impact on the informality issue related to offshore insurances in that case, given that it cannot be written outside Costa Rica even under the legal clauses for countries with trade agreements. Similarly, there is a 5.5 percent withholding tax on reinsurance premiums ceded to reinsurers not domiciled in Costa Rica.

13. *Reglamento sobre Autorizaciones, Registros y Requisitos de Funcionamiento de Entidades Supervisadas por la Superintendencia General de Seguros* issued by CONASSIF in September 2012 permitted "paired" or "free discussion" insurance in marine hull, aviation, railway vehicles, cargo, fire and allied perils, and third-party liability provided that the insurers are registered for the relevant class of business and the premium exceeds UD 200,000 (*unidad de desarrollo*, around US$315,000). These insurances are reported to SUGESE.

14. For example, the INS separated the previously operated fire service. It also announced it was to sell its pension fund operator in June 2012 to merge it with BCR Pensiones, an operation of Banco de Costa Rica.

CHAPTER 4

Telecommunications and the End of Another Monopoly

Eloy Vidal

Introduction and Summary

The Dominican Republic–Central America–United States Free Trade Agreement (CAFTA-DR) agreement opened the door for private investments in the telecommunications sector. A new telecommunications law was required for the liberalized market; a new regulator, the Superintendency of Telecommunications (*Superintendencia de Telecomunicaciones* [SUTEL]), needed to be established and to develop its procedures and functions; and the Costa Rican Electricity Institute (*Instituto Costarricense de Electricidad* [ICE])—which was the existing monopoly provider at that time—needed to adjust to the new environment. Prior to liberalization, the telecommunications sector experienced supply constraints, with a large unmet demand for mobile telephone services and very high prices for Internet access.

Market penetration was rising before liberalization, but the market has shown extraordinary growth in access and price reduction after liberalization. Competition led to an abundant supply of services and a dramatic reduction in prices for Internet access, and Costa Ricans have responded by subscribing massively to the new services. New entrants have become established and are actively competing with the ICE, which is responding to the competitive landscape with its own strategies. All indicators demonstrate that after liberalization, Costa Rica is well positioned in comparison with Latin American countries of similar GDP per capita. Today consumers can buy a cell line instantly, without the long waits that were prevalent prior to liberalization. As well, the telecommunications sector's contribution to the GDP increased substantially. The sector attracted large foreign direct investment (FDI) flows, produced a significant consumer surplus advantage from the reduction in prices and increase in Internet and cellular line access, and made an important contribution to economic growth.

However, as the experience of telecommunications liberalization in other countries would lead one to expect, some issues remain. In Costa Rica, these issues are partly due to the fact that the government still owns the largest telecommunications operator, which is not typical of the majority of Latin American countries. Four important challenges remain: liberalizing rates to allow for sufficient investment, broadening spectrum access to enable improved service, facilitating infrastructure sharing and municipal permits, and ensuring universal access by reforming the activities of the National Telecommunications Fund (*Fondo Nacional de Telecomunicaciones* [FONATEL]).

This chapter presents a summary of the main legislative changes, trends in access with international comparisons, and a discussion of prices and service quality. Conclusions and policy recommendations are included in the final section.

Legal and Regulatory Developments

CAFTA-DR committed Costa Rica to liberalizing its telecommunications market.[1] Costa Rica committed to allow telecommunications providers to compete, through the technology of their choice, in private network, Internet, and mobile wireless services. CAFTA-DR also required the prevention of any anticompetitive practice and the provision of reasonable and nondiscriminatory access to submarine cable facilities. In terms of regulatory principles, CAFTA-DR mandated the establishment of a new independent regulator and transparency in interconnection agreements, procedures for licensing, and authorizations. Furthermore, the procedures for the allocation and use of limited resources, such as frequencies, should be objective, timely, transparent, and nondiscriminatory. And the interconnection among public telecommunications suppliers should be nondiscriminatory and cost-oriented.

In 2008, the new telecommunications law provided the key mechanism for liberalization. The *Ley General de Telecomunicaciones* was enacted as Law No. 8642 on June 30, 2008. The law ended the monopoly of ICE in the telecommunications sector and allowed the entry of private companies. The same law created a new regulator, SUTEL. SUTEL started operations on January 2009, with a mandate to resolve monopolistic practices,[2] set tariffs in the form of price caps to stimulate competition and efficiency, and regulate interconnection of operators' networks, based on cost-oriented rates.

The law assigned to the executive responsibility for planning and administering the radio spectrum, and for awarding new frequency bands. Operators could gain access to the market through: (a) *concessions*, for services that have commercial use and require the use of radio-electric spectrum, granted through public auction; (b) *authorizations*, for commercial or private network services that do not require spectrum, granted through direct request to SUTEL; and (c) *permits*, for noncommercial, official, navigation, or emergency services, granted by the executive through SUTEL. To continue the goal of universal access and reduce the digital divide, the law created FONATEL to provide funds for priority projects. FONATEL is financed by fees from operators as determined by SUTEL,[3] as well as fines, grants, and interest generated by its resources.

Spectrum, privacy, and numbering regulations were enacted.[4] The Regulatory Authority of Public Services (*Autoridad Reguladora de los Servicios*

Públicos [ARESEP]) issued regulations that defined the methodology for setting rates. SUTEL would initially set rates until conditions allowed for effective competition in a specific market, at which point operators would be free to set their own rates.[5] For the initial determination, SUTEL should use a price cap methodology based on long-term incremental costs (LRIC).[6] Since this regulation was approved, SUTEL has maintained all initial rates at the same level that was approved in 2006 by ARESEP.[7] SUTEL has not declared effective competition in any market yet. This decision will have an important impact on operators, as discussed in the next section.

The law also affected radio and television broadcastings as well as the radio spectrum. It modified the *Ley de Radio*,[8] and a transitory provision[9] required public and private concessionaires of frequency bands to report to the executive the use of each one of them. The executive could then request them to return the frequency bands that needed to be reassigned. However, the government has not completed this reassignment yet. ICE still holds the largest share of the mobile frequency bands, giving it a competitive advantage.

In 2008, the Legislative Assembly approved another law changing important elements of the sector structure (see figure 4.1). The so-called ICE law[10] initially defined the Ministry of Environment, Energy and Telecommunications (*Ministerio de Ambiente, Energía y Telecomunicaciones* [MINAET]) as the sector's head, by the addition of a new Vice Ministry of Telecommunications. This put MINAET in charge of formulating public policies, planning, and awarding concessions for the sector, among other functions. The Chinchilla Administration later moved this Vice Ministry to the newly created Ministry of Science, Technology and Telecommunications (*Ministerio de Ciencia, Tecnología, y Telecomunicaciones* [MICITT]) in January 2013. It also modified the law governing ARESEP[11] to make SUTEL a part of that agency.[12] In addition to the functions described above, SUTEL is in charge of supervising the use of the radio spectrum, as well as the obligations and rights of users and telecommunications operators. SUTEL's governance structure consists of three council members, who are appointed by ARESEP's Board of Directors and approved by the Legislative Assembly for five year-terms.[13]

The ICE Law also eliminated some restrictions to allow ICE to compete against private companies in the telecommunications sector. It included the following provisions, among others: (a) allowed ICE to form subsidiaries, national or international, and to form strategic alliances with private or public companies; (b) restricted concessions of fixed telephone service;[14] (c) removed the government's financial restrictions on ICE; (d) allowed ICE to increase its debt level up to 45 percent of total assets; (e) specified new procurement procedures;[15] and (f) gave ICE's board the authority to manage its own human resource administration, including setting staff salaries and benefits. The authorization for ICE to form strategic alliances with private companies is especially important, because these alliances could bring capital, entrepreneurship, and management experience to improve ICE's capacity and competitiveness.

Figure 4.1 Sector Structure before and after CAFTA-DR

Before CAFTA-DR (2008)	After CAFTA-DR (2012)
M i n i s t r y		

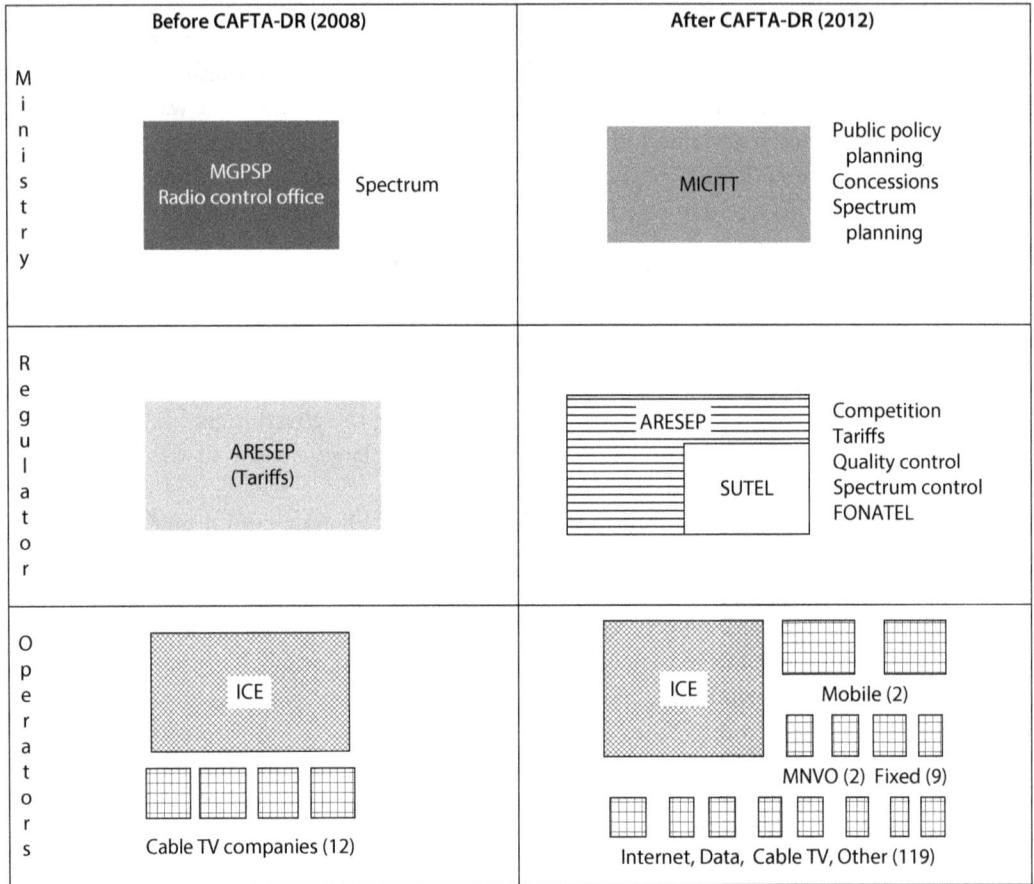

Source: SUTEL 2013.
Note: ARESEP Regulatory Authority of Public Services (*Autoridad Reguladora de los Servicios Públicos*); FONATEL = National Telecommunications Fund (*Fondo Nacional de Telecomunicaciones*); ICE = Costa Rican Electricity Institute (*Instituto Costarricense de Electricidad*); MGPSP = Ministry of Interior, Justice and Public Security (*Ministerio de Gobernación, Justicia y Seguridad Pública*); MICITT = Ministry of Science, Technology and Telecommunications (*Ministerio de Ciencia, Tecnología y Telecomunicaciones*); MINAET = Ministry of Environment, Energy and Telecommunications (*Ministerio de Ambiente, Energía y Telecomunicaciones*); MNVO= mobile network virtual operator; SUTEL = Superintendency of Telecommunications (*Superintendencia de Telecomunicaciones*).

The Entry of Private Mobile Service Providers

Private mobile services providers entered the market in November 2011. After a public auction managed by SUTEL, the government granted two concessions of frequency bands for mobile services in January to Empresa Claro Costa Rica Telecomunicaciones[16] (Claro) and Telefónica[17] (Movistar) (see table 4.1). These concessions included obligations to deploy infrastructure. The criteria for selecting districts to be covered in Phases One, Two, and Three were based on coverage, population, and Human Development Index (HDI) (see table 4.2). Companies had to roll out their networks in 12 months for the San José Metropolitan Area

Table 4.1 Concessions for Mobile Telecommunications Service, US$

Concessionaire	Price paid	Band	Segment	Bandwidth, MHz
Claro	$75 million	1,800 MHz	C	2 × 5
			D	2 × 15
		2,100 MHz	C	2 × 5
			D	2 × 10
Movistar	$95 million	850 MHz	E	2 × 5.3
		1,800 MHz	E	2 × 10
		2,100 MHz	E	2 × 10 MHz

Source: Based on data from Superintendency of Telecommunications (*Superintendencia de Telecomunicaciones*) SUTEL.
Note: MHz = megahertz.

Table 4.2 Phases and Criteria for Cellular Concessions in Costa Rica

Phase	Months	Criteria for selecting districts			Number of districts	Roads (P—primary S—secondary)
		Coverage by the incumbent	Population	Human development index		
1—GAM[a]	12	= Incumbent	>= GAM average	>= GAM average	132 (28%)	GAM: P,S
2—Rest of country	36	= Incumbent	>= Country average	>= Rest of the country average	185 (40%)	Rest of the country: P
3—Rest of country	60	= Incumbent	>= Country average	All	128 (27%)	Rest of the country: S
4—Not covered	n.a.	n.a.	n.a.	n.a.	21 (5%)	n.a.
High signal[b]	n.a.	n.a.	n.a.	n.a.	466 (100%)	n.a.

Source: Superintendency of Telecommunications (*Superintendencia de Telecomunicaciones*) SUTEL 2010. Appendix A *Obligaciones de Cobertura Mínima*).
Note: n.a. = not applicable.
a. GAM = Greater Metropolitan Area of the Central Valley of Costa Rica, as defined by the Regional and Urban Plan for the Greater Metropolitan Area of the Central Valley of Costa Rica (*Planificación Regional y Urbana de la Gran Área Metropolitana del Valle Central de Costa Rica* [PRUGAM]), and includes districts in the Alajuela, Cartago, Heredia, and San Jose provinces.
b. Signal strength must be higher than 75 decibel-milliwatts in those areas.

(Phase One), 36 months for Phase Two, and 60 months for Phase Three. As can be seen in table 4.2, the majority of the country was included in Phase Three. The districts not included have very low population density, are mountainous, or are located in national reserves.

Claro and Movistar had delays in installing their systems due to the slow approval of tower building permits by the municipalities. Although this problem was partially resolved on November 16, 2011, by a ruling of the Supreme Court,[18] some municipalities delayed granting the permits, arguing that they had to issue tower construction regulations first. For example, at the time of writing this report, Claro had not obtained permits from eight municipalities.[19]

Due to difficulties in obtaining construction permits, private mobile providers had to request an extension to complete Phase One of their rollout plans (see table 4.2). SUTEL granted the extension through early February 2014. In spite of these difficulties, Claro and Movistar were able to expand their coverage to near 90 percent of the coverage of Phase Three.[20] The companies have installed masts in buildings, signs, and other existing structures. They have even used portable installations instead of towers to provide coverage. These practices have resulted in extending coverage almost nationwide in a shorter period of time than originally agreed to under their contracts. While this solved the immediate need to provide service, the companies are concerned about meeting their coverage obligations in terms of signal strength, because these solutions, while innovative, do not seem to provide the same signal strength as towers of the height and location specified in the original engineering designs.

Liberalization Drives Improvements in Access to Telecommunications Services

Since 2009, the number of mobile-cellular lines increased markedly, as operators expanded their infrastructure to meet demand (see figure 4.2). ICE launched its 3G network in anticipation of competition purchased with a system

Figure 4.2 Mobile Cellular Lines in Costa Rica, 2003–12

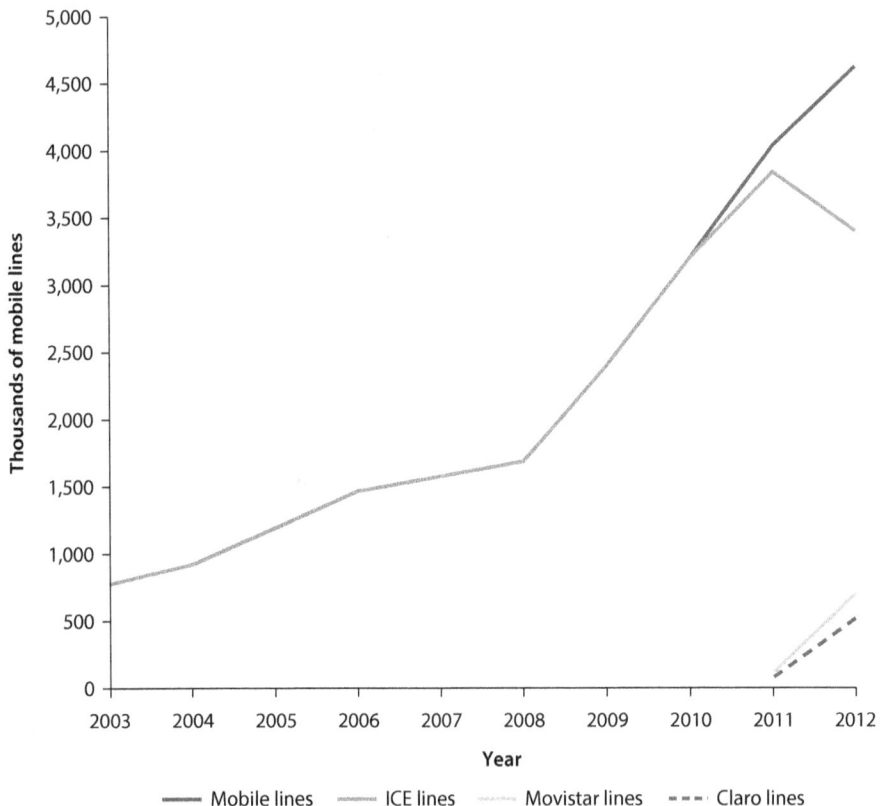

Source: Based on data from Wireless Intelligence.
Note: ICE = Costa Rican Electricity Institute (Instituto Costarricense de Electricidad).

from Huawei.[21] This was the first nationwide mobile system of modern technology that allowed users to connect to the Internet, and replaced several obsolete systems that ICE had in operation. Even though ICE significantly increased lines compared with 2008, it lost market share of about one million lines to Claro and Movistar in 2012.

Mobile cellular penetration levels have quickly caught up with other countries in the region. As operators expanded their coverage to meet unsatisfied demand for services, mobile cellular penetration levels increased from 42 percent in 2008 to 116 percent in 2012 (see figure 4.3). Costa Rica ranks favorably in the region; it has better penetration than Peru and Colombia and is close to that of Uruguay and Guatemala.[22] Today consumers can buy a cell line instantly, whereas before liberalization it took months to get a cellular line. This is a major achievement of sector liberalization due to CAFTA-DR, and has benefited consumers and businesses in Costa Rica.

Figure 4.3 Mobile Cellular Lines per 100 Inhabitants, Costa Rica and Selected Countries, 2003–12

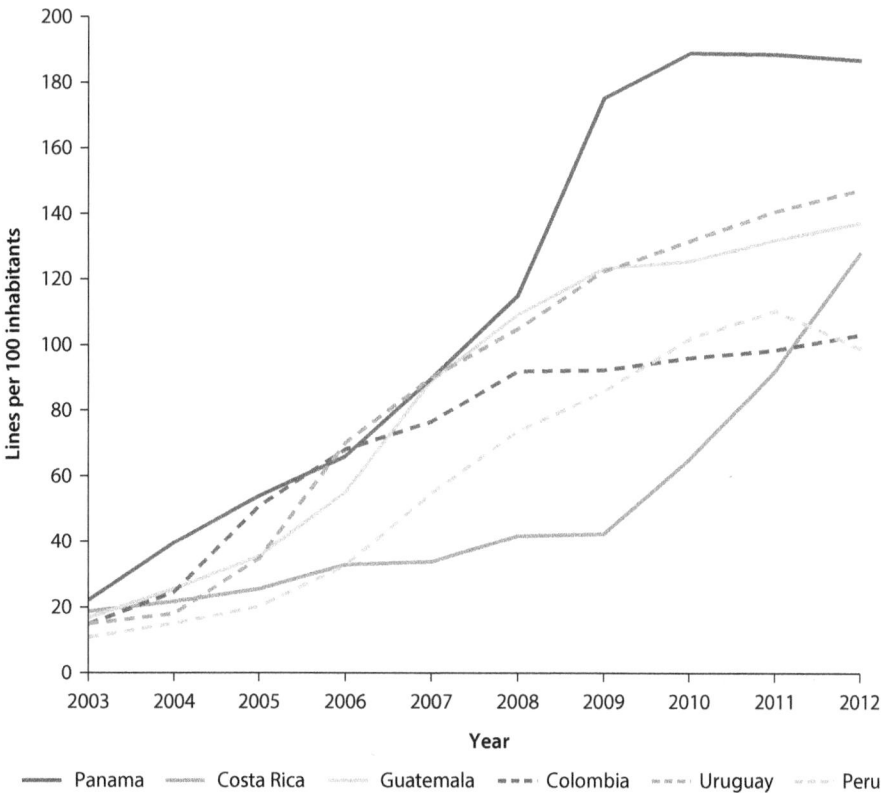

Source: Based on data from World Development Indicators.

Fixed-Line Telephone Services

Costa Rica continues to have a high penetration of fixed lines. This is the result of ICE's investment in its universal service program during the 1970s and 1980s. However, starting in 2010, some users disconnected their fixed lines, reversing the growing trend of the past, due to (a) substitution of mobile for fixed-line service and (b) as more people have broadband Internet access, they prefer use of VoIP (voice over Internet protocol).[23] These trends are common in all countries (see figure 4.4). The reduction in the number of lines in operation impacts ICE's finances, as ICE is the sole provider of fixed telephone services; revenues have decreased while operating expenses have continued to grow due to the labor-intensive nature of maintaining the old copper network.

Fixed Internet

Fixed Internet connections have increased exponentially (see figure 4.5). During the monopoly period, cable companies were forced to rent wholesale Internet access from *Radiográfica Costarricense, S.A.* (RACSA), an ICE subsidiary that, in

Figure 4.4 Fixed Telephone Lines per 100 Inhabitants, Costa Rica and Selected Countries, 2003–12

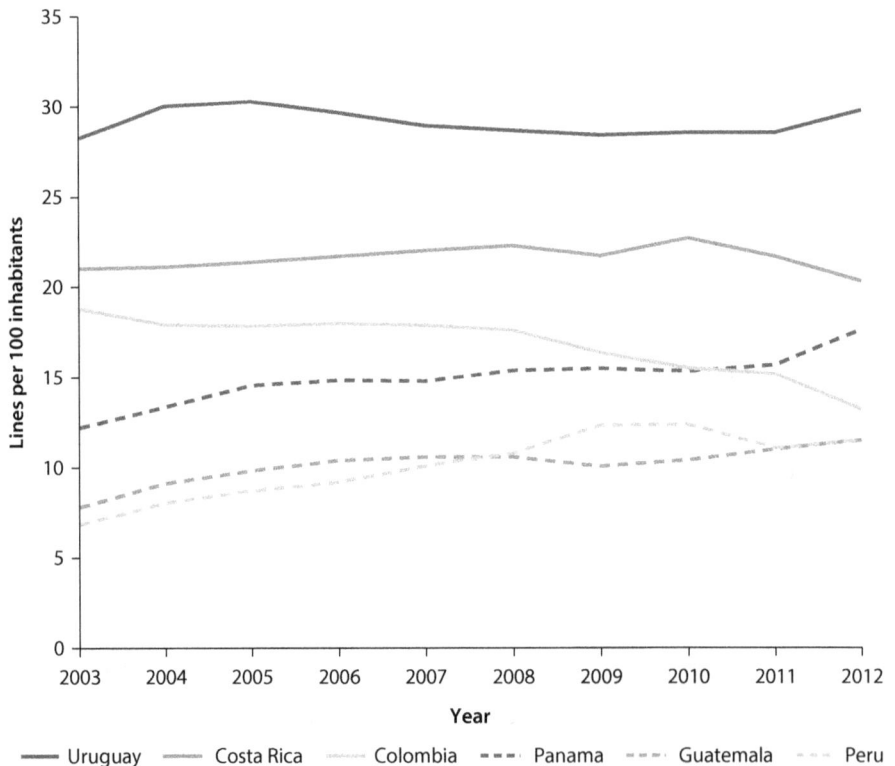

Sources: Data for Costa Rica from *Programa Estado de la Nación* for 2003–09 and SUTEL (2013) for years 2010–2012; data for other countries from World Development Indicators.

Costa Rica Five Years after CAFTA-DR • http://dx.doi.org/10.1596/978-1-4648-0568-4

Figure 4.5 Fixed Internet Connections in Costa Rica, 2006–12

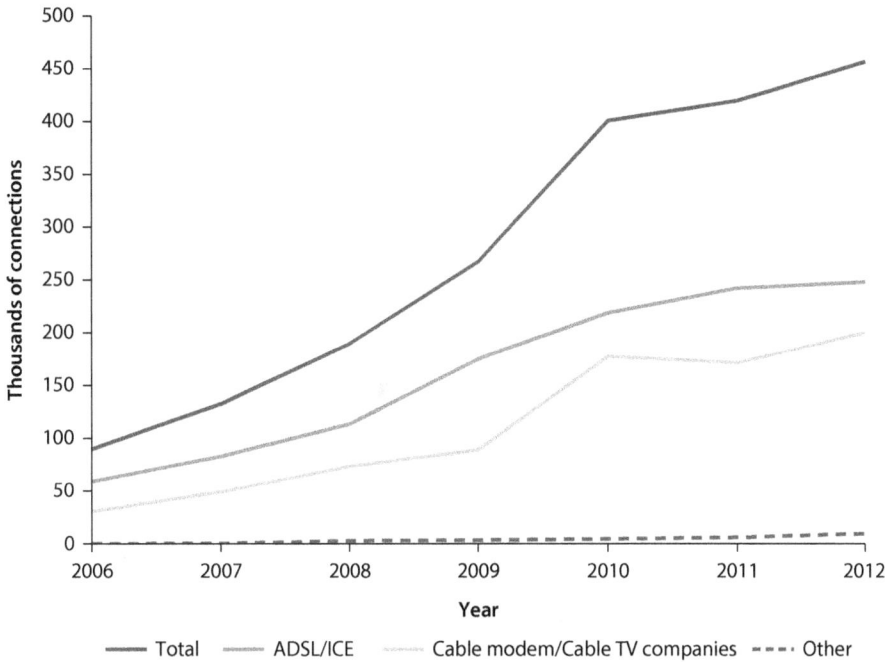

Sources: Data from CISCO Barómetro (2009) for 2006–09 and SUTEL (2013) for 2010–12.
Note: ADSL = asymmetric digital subscriber line; ICE = Costa Rican Electricity Institute (Instituto Costarricense de Electricidad).

turn, leased its bandwidth capacity from the international submarine cable providers. After liberalization, the ability to lease or purchase bandwidth directly from the international providers allowed the cable companies to reduce costs and increase capacity, freeing resources to invest in connecting more subscribers and offering higher connection speeds. ICE responded by increasing the asymmetric digital subscriber line (ADSL)[24] services on its extensive copper infrastructure. Even though ADSL is still the preferred access service, cable modem provided by private cable companies has increased significantly. After 2010, the market started to show saturation, as the majority of households in urban areas were connected to the Internet.

Penetration rates to fixed Internet services improved markedly. Measured by penetration (lines per 100 inhabitants), Costa Rica had 2 percent penetration in 2006, third in its group (after Panama and Uruguay). By 2012, penetration for fixed Internet in Costa Rica increased to 9.5 percent, the second highest (Uruguay had 16.6 percent) surpassing Colombia, Panama, and Peru (see figure 4.6).

Mobile Broadband Services

Mobile broadband connections have quickly expanded, and private operations have captured a large part of the market. In anticipation of competition, ICE introduced mobile broadband services in 2009 (Cordero Perez 2009). Claro and

Figure 4.6 Fixed Internet Connections per 100 Inhabitants, Costa Rica and Selected Countries, 2003–12

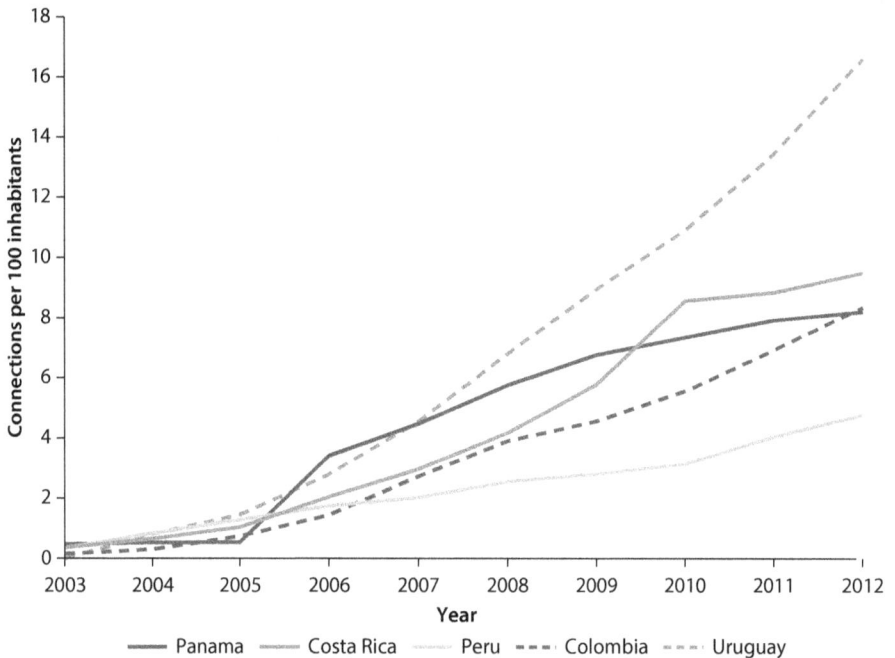

Source: Based on data from World Development Indicators.

Movistar introduced mobile broadband with the opening of their commercial operations and have more subscribers than ICE (see figure 4.7). The three operators use 3G technology (high speed packet access [HSPA+]), allowing them to provide medium-speed broadband access. A recent survey indicates that 61 percent of subscribers use Internet on their personal computers, mobile phones, and other electronic devices. In the face of competition, ICE has become more customer oriented and introduced a variety of new plans and smartphones to the market, like the iPhone and Galaxy,[25] among others.

This rapid growth in connections moved Costa Rica ahead of selected countries in Latin America in terms of penetration. Costa Rica's penetration of mobile broadband was at 0.17 percent in 2009, the lowest of this group (see figure 4.8). By 2012, however, it was the second highest, at nearly 20 percent (Uruguay was 28 percent), as a result of the market growth in the years after CAFTA-DR was approved.

Household Access to Telecommunications Services, Prices, and Quality of Services

Costa Rica climbed five positions in the Global Information Technology Report 2013 of the World Economic Forum, to 53rd of 144 countries. This compares favorably with position 60 in 2007 (of 127 countries). In Latin America it was

Figure 4.7 Mobile Broadband Connections in Costa Rica, 2009–12

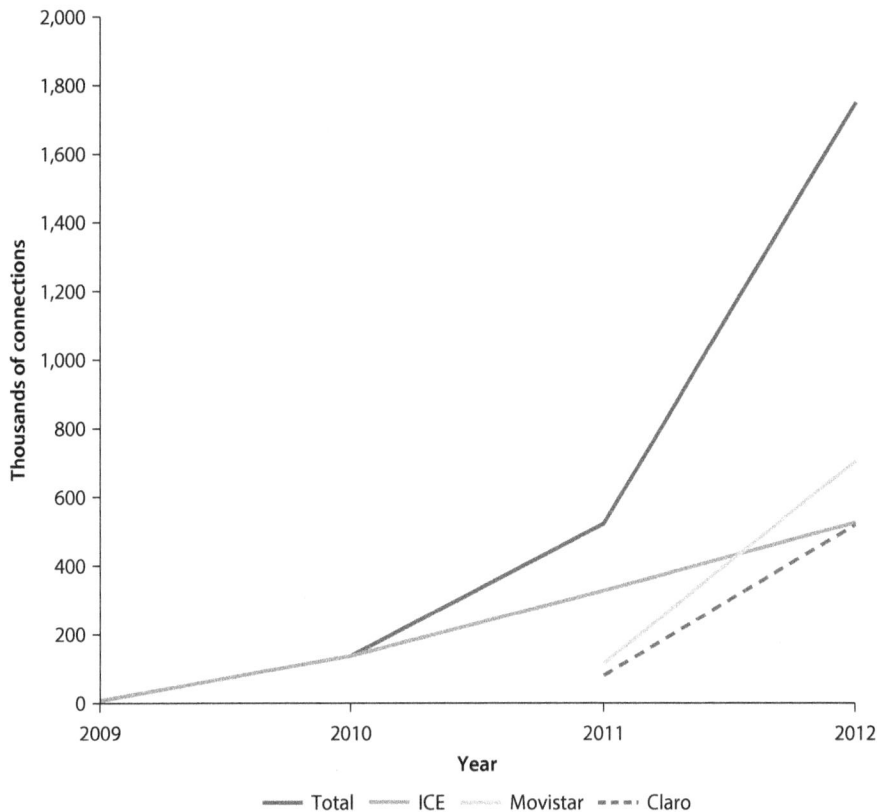

Source: Based on data from Wireless Intelligence.
Note: ICE = Costa Rican Electricity Institute (Instituto Costarricense de Electricidad).

surpassed only by Chile (34), Barbados (39), Panama (46), and Uruguay (52). The report states: "Costa Rica, together with Panama, remains the leader in Information and Communication Technology (ICT) uptake in Central America and climbs five positions in the rankings to 53rd place. Overall, the country has continued its efforts to develop its very affordable (6th) ICT infrastructure, especially in terms of improving its international Internet bandwidth capacity (40th) that, coupled with a well-performing educational system (21st), allows for an overall strong ICT readiness (33rd)."

An increasing number of households are using telecom services in Costa Rica. The proportion of households with Internet access has increased from 10 percent in 2006 to 47 percent in 2013, which corresponds to a 30 percent annual average growth rate (see figure 4.9). In the same period, 22 percent of households gained access to mobile phone services, and 16 percent to cable TV. Although cable TV has always been provided by private companies, liberalization of Internet access

Figure 4.8 Mobile Broadband Connections per 100 Inhabitants, Costa Rica and Selected Countries, 2005–12

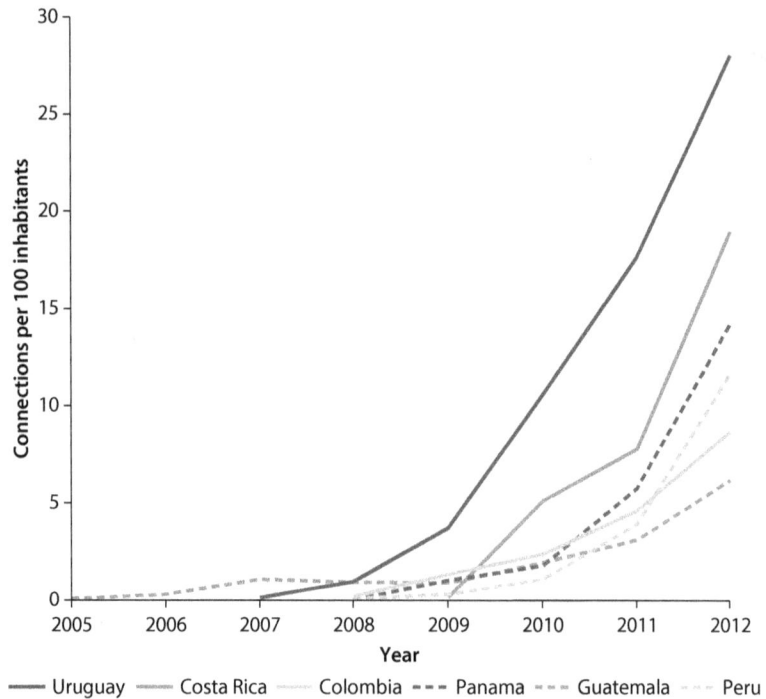

Source: Data for Costa Rica comes from SUTEL 2013 and data for other countries comes from Wireless Intelligence.

increased competition among public and private companies, who began to offer bundled services like double play (TV and Internet) and triple play (voice, TV, and Internet).

Fixed Internet Services

After liberalization, operators introduced higher-speed Internet access offers and bundled packages. Download speeds for fixed Internet access increased significantly in the period from 2009 to 2012 (see figure 4.10). In 2008, 52 percent of connections were less than 512 Kbps (kilobits per second) and in 2012 this service level dropped to only 2 percent. During the same period, faster connections of more than 2 Mbps (megabits per second) increased from 9 percent to 53 percent. A higher access speed is essential for a better user experience and to enable the use of services like video streaming, video conferencing and large file sharing. Although download speeds in Costa Rica are still below those in Organisation for Economic Co-operation and Development (OECD) countries, the trend toward higher speeds is irreversible. Faster Internet connections are especially needed by IT-intensive businesses such as IT help desks, software development centers,

Figure 4.9 Usage of Telecommunications Services in Costa Rica

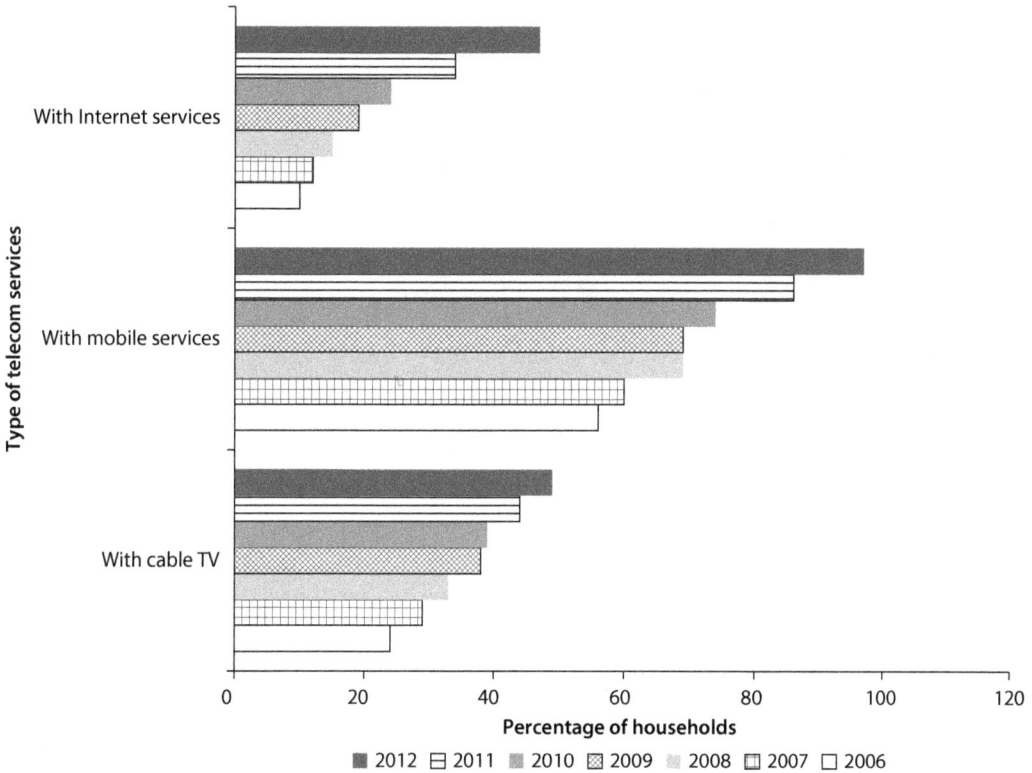

Source: Data from MICITT 2013 using data from National Institute of Statistics and Census (*Instituto Nacional de Estadísticas y Censos* [INEC]).

e-commerce, and e-services; companies involved in outsourcing, banking, insurance, and consulting need fast Internet connections as well.

Internet prices in Costa Rica are relatively low compared to other countries (see figure 4.11). Before 2006, ICE offered low-speed Internet access at high prices that were too expensive for poor households.[26] In anticipation of liberalization, ICE reduced prices for high-speed service (*Acelera*) in 2009. Even though price caps for Internet access were set relatively high, competition between ICE and cable TV companies has reduced prices and increased speeds. Data from August 2013 indicate prices well below the price caps fixed by ARESEP and SUTEL (see table 4.3).

Mobile Services

Increased penetration in mobile services is explained by the introduction of prepaid mobile cellular service and low tariffs. Compared to other countries and other operators, ICE was late to introduce prepaid services in April 2008.[27] Claro and Movistar offered them from the start of their operations in

Figure 4.10 Fixed Internet Download Speeds in Costa Rica, 2007–12

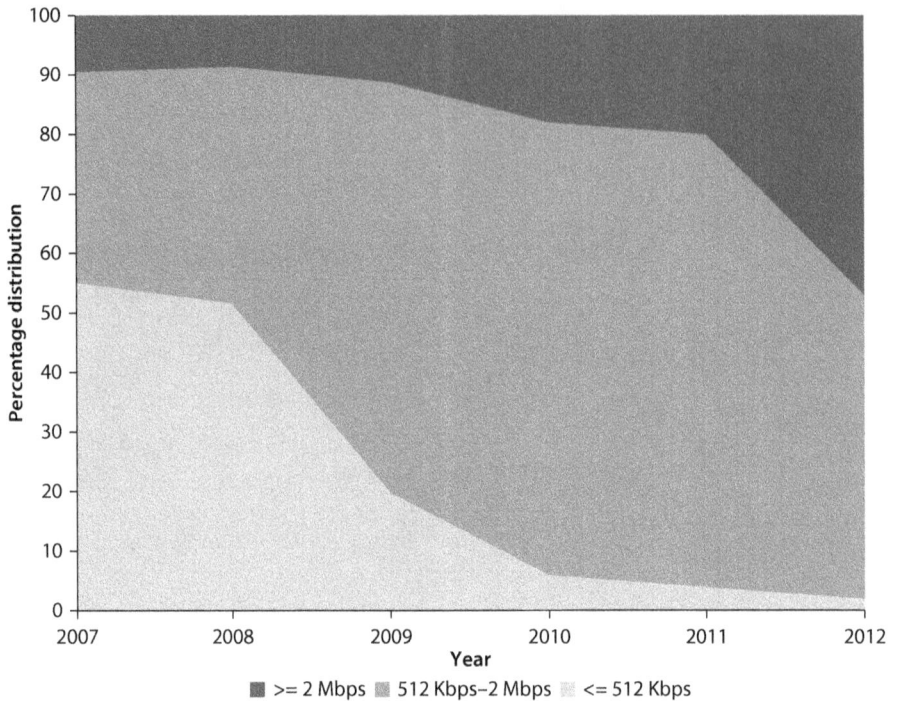

Sources: Based on data from CISCO Barómetro 2009 and SUTEL 2013.
Note: Kbps = kilobits per second; Mbps = megabits per second.

November 2011. Prepaid services are very popular in Latin America, especially for the lower-income quintiles of the population, because they allow users to control expenditures and purchase service in small incremental amounts. The other key driver for growth was the low prepaid tariffs set by ARESEP (see tables 4.4 and 4.5). The prices are low when compared to other countries in Latin America (see figure 4.12). This figure compares peak rates only, without figuring in any discounts or promotions.[28] Even though promotions are not reflected in the graph, it is fair to say that Costa Rica, in general, has some of the lowest rates in Latin America; this, in addition to control and convenience, induced more users to select prepaid plans. While there were no prepaid users in 2007, 49 percent of users selected prepaid plans in 2010, and 79 percent in 2012.

Mobile rates continue to be fixed at the rates set by ARESEP in 2006, and as a result they have lost value in real terms. These tariffs remain valid as price caps,[29] with the exception of the tariff for off-peak service. If the tariffs were adjusted by inflation, the "equivalent tariffs" in 2012 *colones* would have been substantially higher (see table 4.5). All operators introduced several plans that are in line with the rates. Cellular rates in most countries are deregulated, as operators compete with different plans and packages that offer phones and a set

Figure 4.11 Fixed Internet Prices of One Mbps, Selected Countries, 2012

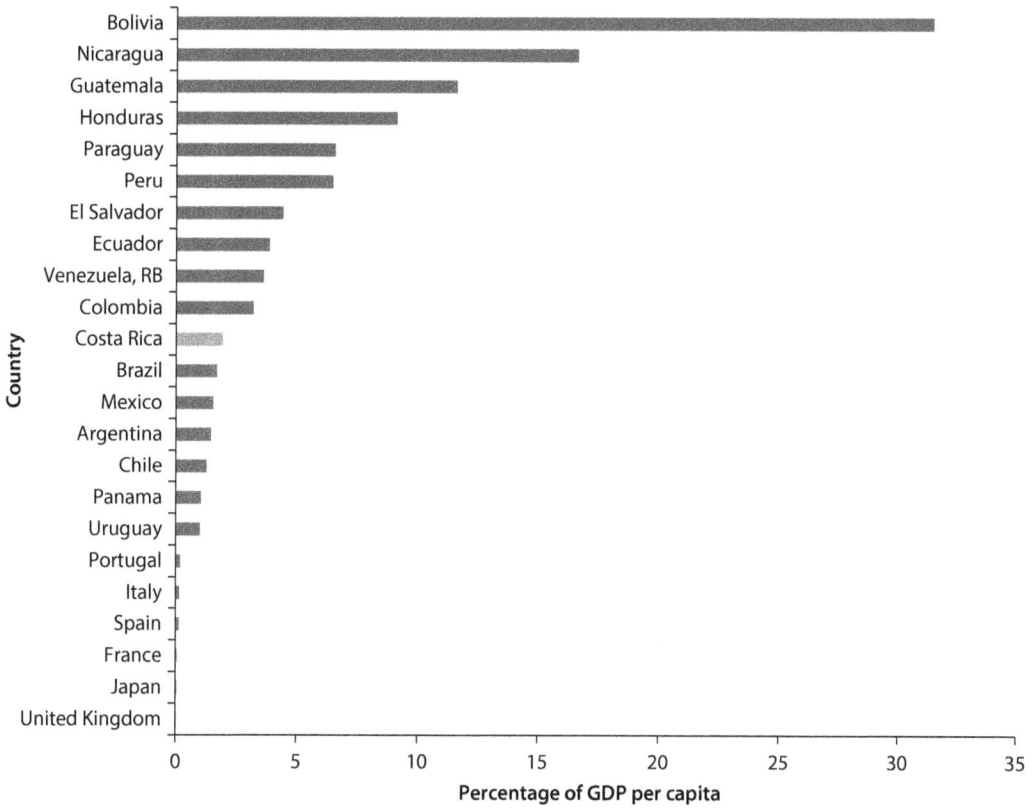

Source: ORBA 2012.
Note: Mbps = megabits per second.

Table 4.3 Fixed Internet Prices in Costa Rica, US$ per Month, August 2013

Download speed	TIGO	Cable Tica	ICE-Kolbi	RACSA
1 Mbps	16.95	16.50	18.90	30.00
2 Mbps	20.95	19.90	27.90	40.00
3 Mbps	29.95	28.90	—	—
4 Mbps	38.95	—	48.90	—
5 Mbps	49.95	48.60	—	—
10 Mbps	90.95	87.50	98.90	—

Sources: Information retrieved from http://www.tigo.cr (*Plan Hogar, Estandar,* Plus, Deluxe, Pro, Extreme, Ultra); http://www.cabletica.com (*Basico, Estandar,* Plus, Silver, Gold); http://www.grupoice.com (*Kolbi Hogar*); and http://www.racsa.co.cr (WiMax Plus, Premium).
Note: ICE = Costa Rican Electricity Institute (*Instituto Costarricense de Electricidad*); Mbps = megabits per second; RACSA = *Radiográfica de Costa Rica;* — = not available.

Table 4.4 Cellular Prepaid Rates, US$, 2008

	Prepaid plan (US$)		
	5	10	20
Valid for (days)	30	45	60
Price, cents/minute, peak	8.00	7.40	6.80
Price, cents/minute, reduced (night and weekend rates)	6.40	6.00	5.60
Price, SMS, cents	0.34	0.34	0.34

Source: ARESEP (Regulatory Authority of Public Services [*Autoridad Reguladora de los Servicios Públicos*]), Resolution 8147-2008.
Note: US$1.00 = CRC 500. SMS = set number of minutes.

Table 4.5 Tariffs, Prices, and Equivalent Tariffs for Selected Services

	Tariffs		Prices		
	2006	2012	2006	2012	Equivalent tariff
Cellular	(2006 CRC)		(2006 CRC)		(2012 CRC)
Prepaid plan CRC 2,500 (US$5), per minute		26.08		26.08	49.41
Postpaid, per month	2,900	1,890.81	2,900	1,890.81	4,447.84
Postpaid, peak, per minute	30	19.56	30	19.56	46.01
Internet access, per month (unlimited)	3,500	2,282.01	3,500	2,282.01	5,368.08
Fixed telephone	(2006 CRC)		(2006 CRC)		(2012 CRC)
Rent, residential, per month (includes 160 minutes)	1,850	1,206.20	1,850	1,206.20	2,837.41
Rent, commercial, per month (includes 160 minutes)	2,150	1,401.81	2,150	1,401.81	3,297.53
Calls, peak, per minute (from 7 AM to 7 PM)	4.10	2.67	4.10	2.67	6.29
Fixed Internet access, US$ per month	(2006 US$)		(2006 US$)		(2012 US$)
1 Mbps	38	33.40	38	14.50	43.23
2 Mbps	91	79.98	91	17.58	103.54

Sources: ARESEP (Regulatory Authority of Public Services [*Autoridad Reguladora de los Servicios Públicos*]), Resolution RRG—5957-2006 published in *La Gaceta*, September 25, 2006, and for operators' website for fixed Internet access.
Note: Equivalent tariff is the tariff in 2012 currency that has the same real value as the tariff of 2006. Conversion to constant 2006 CRC was made using the Central Bank of Costa Rica consumer price index (CPI) July to July change for each year. Conversion to 2006 US$ was done using the U.S. Department of Labor average-to-average CPI change from year to year. Mbps = megabits per second.

number of minutes (SMS), multimedia messaging system (MMS), and Internet access. The consumer thus has a wide range of options from which to select the best plan and the preferred phone. In this, Costa Rica is an exception. While SUTEL has the authority to deregulate cellular rates, it has not indicated that it will do so in the near future.

Mobile Broadband

An important factor in the high use of mobile broadband has been the flat rate that ARESEP has imposed since the introduction of mobile broadband. This is a fixed rate, irrespective of the usage. Unfortunately, as in many countries, a small

Figure 4.12 Cellular Prepaid Prices in U.S. Cents per Minute, Peak for Latin American Countries, 2010

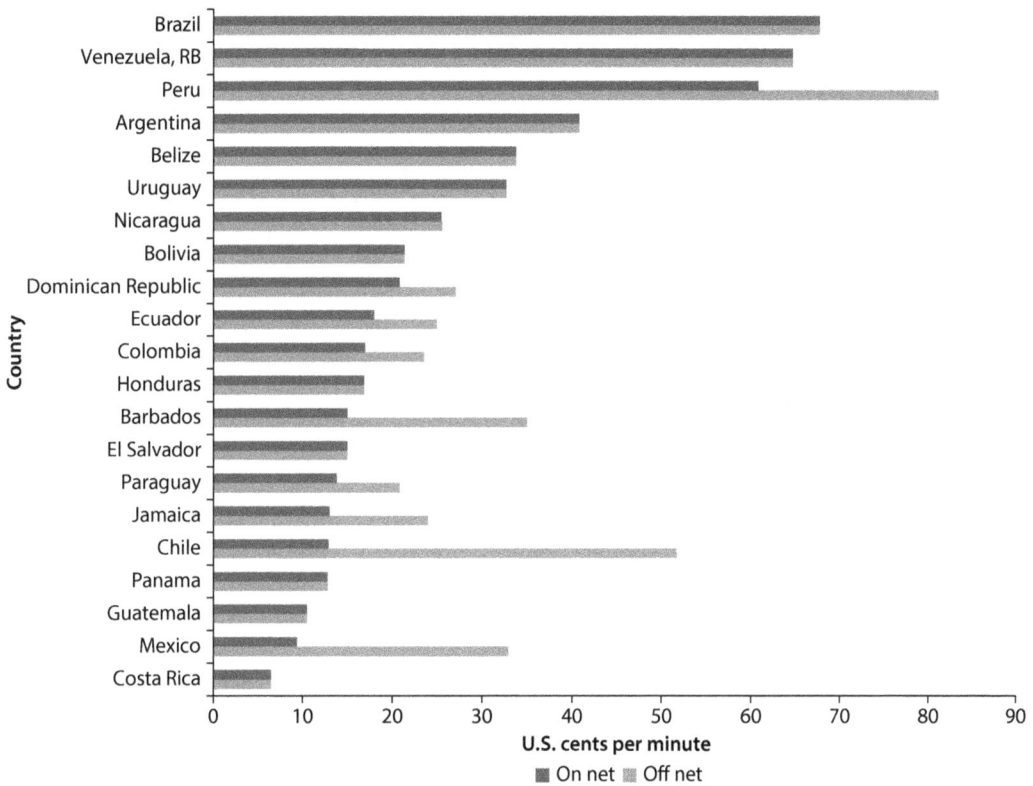

Source: Based on data from World Telecommunication/ICT Indicators database (2012), https://www.itu.int/pub/D-IND-WTID.OL-2013.
Note: These prices do not include promotions. Prepaid services are more expensive per minute (without promotions) when compared with postpaid (contract) services.

percentage of heavy users have congested the networks. Most operators world-wide charge rates per kilobyte (KB) (or megabyte [MB]) to deal with this issue. SUTEL modified the rate, charging a fee per kilobyte of use in October of 2012.[30] Operators started charging CRC 0.0076 (US$0.00152) per kilobyte of use in August 2013. Costa Rican mobile broadband rates are in the middle to low end of Latin American countries in terms of mobile broadband fees (see figure 4.13).[31]

Penetration in Rural Areas versus Urban Areas: FONATEL

As a result of liberalization, telecom services became available in most urban areas of Costa Rica. However, some rural areas and small towns still do not have access to the Internet. To provide services in those areas, the Telecommunications Law created FONATEL. FONATEL has raised US$213 million from auction proceeds and operator's fees (Pineda 2013). FONATEL

Figure 4.13 Mobile Broadband Rates for Selected Countries

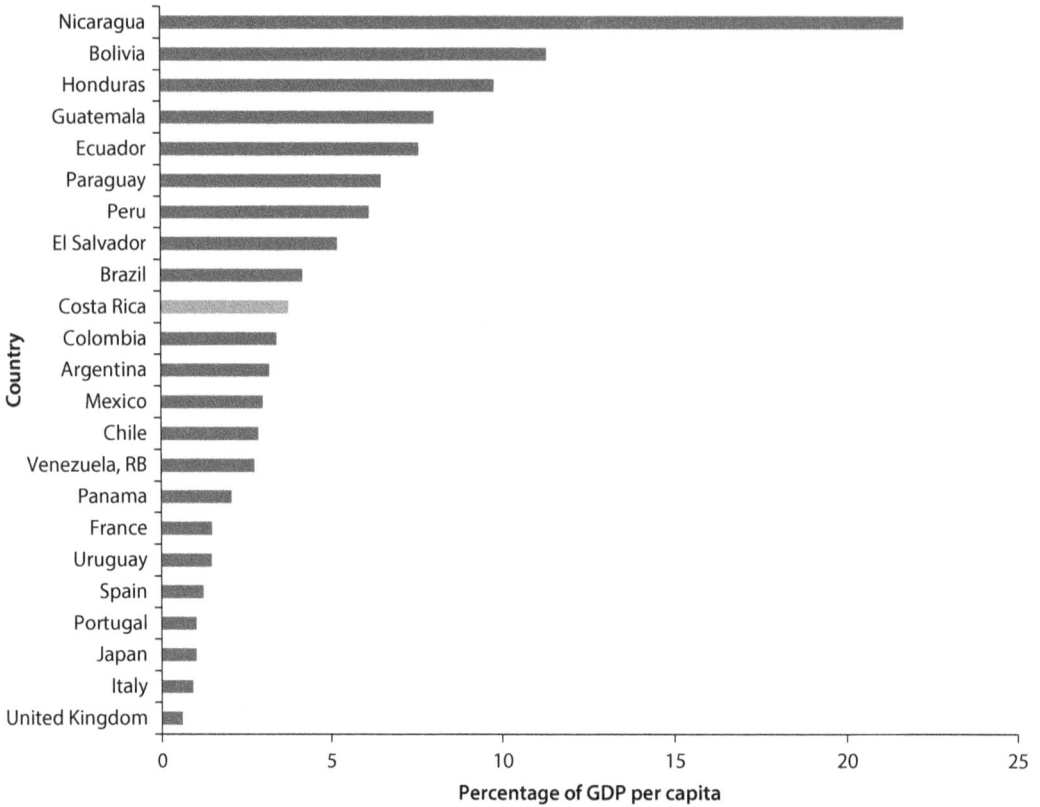

Source: ORBA 2012.

prepared a master plan that includes four programs: (a) *Comunidades Conectadas*, to connect 2,731 communities that do not have access to the Internet at a cost of US$155 million; (b) *Poblaciones Vulnerables*, to provide subsidies to 620,000 disabled or vulnerable people, at a cost of US$50 million; (c) "Equipment for Schools," a program projected to reach 40,000 children at a cost of US$30 million; and (d) a yet to-be-determined program to impose services obligations on telecommunications operators.

Only the first program has been started. FONATEL recently awarded the first bid for *Comunidades Conectadas* in Siquirres. This is a very small pilot project, one of three designed for the Atlantic region, which is the poorest. The northern region was to follow later in 2013. It also awarded the *La Roxana* Project in Pococi in September 2013. Introduction of the program to the southern region was to be completed in early 2014. The less poor Chorotega and central regions are scheduled for late 2014. *Comunidades Conectadas* will provide Internet access to (a) all the population in these towns and villages with up to 2 Mbps connections and (b) schools, health centers, preschool day care centers, and community access centers with up to 4 Mbps each.

The FONATEL program has been criticized because of the long time it has taken SUTEL to create a trust, and to select and contract a management consulting firm to implement the program. It is also criticized for the lack of coordinated investments (for example, computers in schools, health systems and applications, training of teachers and other civil servants) for the ministries of education, health, and others that FONATEL would not finance. SUTEL argues that the law only allowed a maximum of 1 percent of the resources to administer the program, limiting the number of FONATEL staff;[32] that public procurement procedures in Costa Rica are slow and cumbersome; and that cooperation from other ministries has been lacking.

The Contribution of the Telecommunications Sector to the Costa Rican Economy

The telecommunications sector has become an engine of growth in Costa Rica. As a result of CAFTA-DR and sector liberalization, the telecommunications share of GDP increased from 7.3 percent in 2006 to 9.1 percent in 2012 (see figure 4.14). New private companies and ICE contributed more to the value

Figure 4.14 Telecommunications Sector, 2006–12

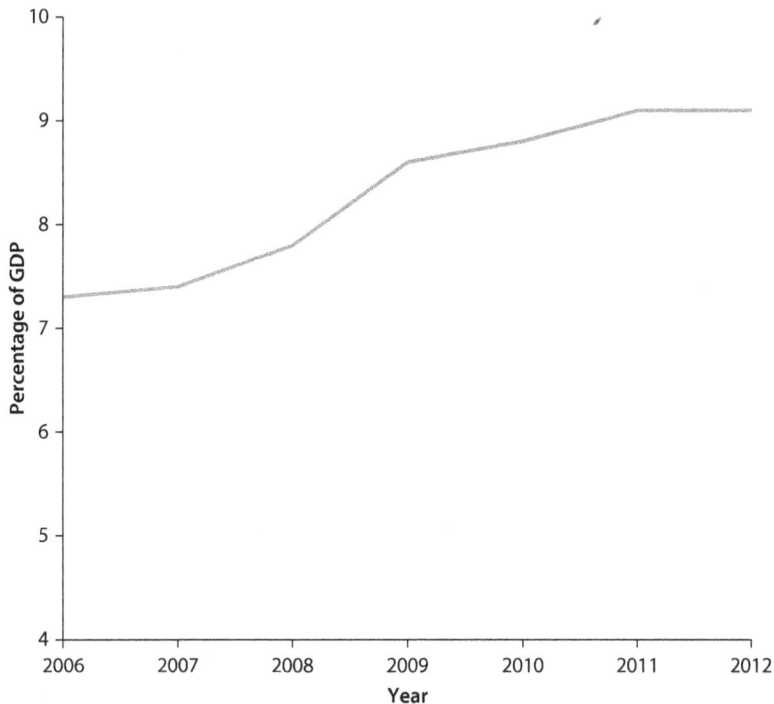

Source: MICITT 2013.

Table 4.6 Estimation of Consumer Surplus for Internet Access Services

Service	Lines		Prices per month (2012 US$)		Consumer surplus (2012 US$)	
	2008	2012	2008	2012	per month	per year
512 Kbps–1 Mbps	42,290	136,918	$40.52	$16.50	$1,136,362	$13,636,338
1 Mbps–2 Mbps	44,593	200,812	$95.96	$24.40	$5,589,701	$67,076,417
>2 Mbps	18,788	50,203	$180.20	$43.90	$2,140,870	$25,690,436
Total	105,671	387,933	n.a.	n.a.	$8,866,933	$106,403,192

Source: Based on data from SUTEL 2013 for lines and prices.
Note: Kbps = kilobits per second; Mbps = megabits per second; n.a. = not applicable. Conversion to 2012 US$ consumer price index for CRC and US$.

added in telecommunications, as they provided more services and added new clients, generating new revenues. FDI in the telecommunications sector was US$339 million in 2011 and US$465 million in 2012.[33]

Competition has generated a consumer surplus. Fixed Internet access prices tumbled from 2008 to 2012. As prices decreased, many Costa Ricans who did not have service began to subscribe and the number of users skyrocketed. The consumer surplus for those consumers was calculated at US$106.4 million in 2012 (see table 4.6).

Improved ICT service has had an economic impact. A positive correlation exists between a country's ICT readiness and its economic competitiveness, and broadband plays an important role in this equation. Numerous studies show the effects on the economies of developed and emerging markets alike. While studies vary in their estimates of broadband's impact on growth, the consensus seems to be that a 10 percent increase in broadband household penetration delivers a boost to a country's GDP that can range between 0.1–1.4 percent.[34] Using these parameters, the estimated economic impact on development for Costa Rica is 9.5 percent of GDP, applying the average of the McKinsey study range (from 1.3 percent to 17.7 percent of GDP; Buttkereit and others 2009), during the period from 2008 to 2012 (a penetration increase of 126 percent).

ICT also generates important social benefits (Kim, Kelly, and Raja 2010). Broadband connects consumers, businesses, and governments and facilitates social interaction (OECD 2009). It delivers information to individuals and businesses, supports good governance, and strengthens social capital. Information about the performance of governments and politicians makes governments more accountable and improves public services. Finally, broadband networks are increasingly used to deliver public services, such as distance education, financial services, health care, electronic voting, and land registration.

Conclusions and Remaining Challenges

The main conclusion of this review is that the telecommunications sector liberalization brought by CAFTA-DR was an outstanding success. Before CAFTA-DR, the sector was a monopoly controlled by ICE. There was considerable unmet demand for mobile telephone services, prices for Internet access were very high—making the service inaccessible for the majority of Costa Ricans—and the sector was supply constrained. After the reforms, increased competition led to an abundant supply of services, prices for Internet access reduced dramatically, and Costa Ricans responded by subscribing massively to the new services. All indicators demonstrate that after sector liberalization Costa Rica is well positioned in comparison with Latin American countries of similar GDP per capita. Finally, the telecommunications sector's contribution to GDP increased substantially. The sector attracted large FDI flows, produced a large consumer surplus advantage from the reduction in prices and increases in quantities of Internet access and cellular lines, and made a large contribution to economic growth.

However, as in any liberalization of the telecommunications sector in any country, some issues remain. In Costa Rica, these issues are partly due to the fact that the government still owns the largest telecommunications operator, which is not typical of the majority of Latin American countries. Four important challenges remain: liberalizing rates to allow for sufficient investment, broadening spectrum access to enable improved service, facilitating infrastructure sharing and municipal permits, and ensuring universal access by reforming the activities of FONATEL.

Rates, Investments, and Sustainability

SUTEL established the initial price caps for cellular services equal to existing rates at the time of liberalization. This means that ICE rates were used as the basis of the price cap levels. This initial rate setting may have had a negative impact on the financial performance of the new cellular private companies, because: (a) unlike its competitors, ICE did not pay for its use of spectrum, and its rates did not reflect this cost; (b) ICE had depreciated assets, like towers, transmission facilities, and buildings, as opposed to the new entrants that had to build every element of their networks from scratch; and (c) interconnection rates may have given ICE a competitive advantage due to the fact that, initially, the majority of the traffic of new entrants' lines was to and from ICE's subscribers, forcing the new entrants to pay for interconnection to ICE, while the majority of ICE's traffic was confined to its own network.

Low price caps on cellular rates restricted investment, because private companies need profits to invest in new technologies, such as 4G LTE, to update the network and provide faster service to users. Therefore, these lower rates are detrimental to promoting investment in the sector. In the majority of Latin American countries and in the world in general, governments do not regulate cellular rates, due to the competitive nature of these markets, where three or more players are actively providing services in a level playing field. In Costa Rica, there are three mobile telecommunications operators and two mobile network virtual operators (MNVOs), for a total of five operators. In many countries, as well as in Costa Rica, operators compete by offering different plans for minutes of voice, set number of minutes (SMS) and megabytes of Internet downloads per month. They offer discounts for on-net, weekends and non-peak hour calls, and many other alternatives. Consumers benefit from a wide choice of plans and services.

SUTEL should consider declaring the market competitive to end rate regulation. Article 50 of the Telecommunications Law gave SUTEL the power to declare whether a specific market is competitive. In a competitive market, SUTEL would no longer regulate rates. As a solution to the current challenge, SUTEL should consider exercising its right to declare this market competitive and end regulation of cellular rates.

Private Operators do not Have Enough Spectrum

Spectrum bands are critical for deploying mobile telecommunications services. As operators deploy new and modern systems to provide faster access to the users, more spectrum is needed. Therefore, the timely award of frequency bands in the quantity and quality[35] required is essential for development of modern mobile services. Today, the majority of countries in Asia, North America, and Europe have awarded frequency bands for 4G LTE, which provides higher-speed Internet access. As a result, operators have deployed their networks and are actively providing this important service to customers. In Latin America, several countries have already awarded bands for 4G, and operators are rolling out the service.

Mobile services in Costa Rica are 3G, which is the previous generation of mobile service. In order to roll out 4G, especially LTE advanced, operators will need additional spectrum. However, when Costa Rica liberalized the telecommunications sector, ICE was the only telecommunications operator. Because of that, the government had assigned 78 percent of mobile spectrum available to ICE (SUTEL 2009). Therefore, on SUTEL's recommendation, MINAET decided to auction three new concessions. Only two were granted, to Claro and Movistar. There were no bidders for the other concession. In addition, Claro does not have lower frequencies, which is a technological and cost disadvantage in comparison with the other two operators, particularly in the provision of services in rural areas.[36] SUTEL also recommended awarding frequencies in the 900 megahertz (MHz) band. This band is occupied by narrow band point-to-point UHF links that can easily migrate to other frequencies. In addition, ICE holds the majority of the 2.5 gigahertz (GHz) band that the International Telecommunication Union recommends for 4G use.[37] ICE plans to roll out LTE in this band in 2014. Another option is using the 700 MHz "digital dividend" band, derived from the transition from analog to digital TV.[38] However, MICITT has announced that this transition will not occur until December 2017. The sooner operators roll out 4G services, the higher the benefits will be for consumers and businesses.

Infrastructure Sharing and Municipal Permits

When Claro and Movistar started building their networks, they were delayed due to the slow process of obtaining construction permits from municipalities. The Sala IV decision and the recent loss of a court case by several municipalities[39] provide reason to hope that this problem will be solved soon. However, as operators roll out 4G in the future, they will probably need to build more towers, and they may encounter delays again. Also, fixed-line operators and cable TV companies need to use ducts and poles to lay fiber. Therefore, this issue has to be resolved. One option is to enforce infrastructure sharing as stated in the law.[40] The recent case of TIGO against JASEC was resolved favorably, as SUTEL forced JASEC to rent its poles to the other company. This precedent may help solve future disputes between new entrants and existing operators over towers, buildings, poles, or ducts sharing, as these elements of the network become critical to deploy new networks.

Universal Service and FONATEL
FONATEL effectiveness needs to be improved to expand access for disadvantaged communities and individuals. FONATEL is finally initiating the program to invest the universal service fund resources to extend service to unconnected communities, schools, health centers, day care centers, and other public community centers in rural areas of Costa Rica. However, it has taken a long time, partly due to the lengthy government procedures established by law. The coordination between FONATEL and the ministries of education, health, and others has not been very effective; and as a result FONATEL has only funded Internet access, leaving to the ministries the financing of computers, local area networks, and the training of students, teachers, vulnerable populations, and government officials. This may result either in ineffective use of the facilities or delays in their use.

Notes

1. See annex 13, "Specific Commitments of Costa Rica on Telecommunications Services," of CAFTA-DR.
2. See Articles 49–61 of the Telecommunications Law.
3. The contribution should be within 1.5 percent and 3.0 percent of the operator gross revenues.
4. *Reglamento a la Ley General de Telecomunicaciones*, No. 34765, *Plan Nacional de Atribución de Frecuencias*, No. 35257, and its reforms in 2010 (No. 35866) and 2011 (No. 36754), *Reglamento sobre Medidas de Protección de la Privacidad de las Comunicaciones*, No. 35205, and *Plan Nacional de Numeración*, No. 35187.
5. The regulation confirms Article 50 of the Telecommunications Law that stipulates these rate-setting principles and elaborates the methodology for setting rates.
6. For the calculation of long-term incremental costs (LRIC), this regulation indicated the formula that must be used and defined its main elements. In particular, the rate of return on investment should not be lower than the national or international average on comparable markets. Comparable markets are defined using criteria such as geographic extension, number of users, quantity of operators providing services, and average income of users.
7. The Regulatory Authority of Public Services (*Autoridad Reguladora de los Servicios Públicos* [ARESEP]), rate setting of 2006 is RRG-5957-2206 of Sept. 25, 2006.

SUTEL's simplification of rates eliminated some of the levels of the previous structure but left most of the core rates intact: RCS-121-2012 of March 30, 2012.

8. Law No. 1758 of June 19, 1954. This law regulates radio and TV broadcasting, and the radio spectrum. The Telecom Law reassigned oversight of the sector to the Ministry of Environment, Energy and Telecommunications (*Ministerio de Ambiente, Energía y Telecomunicaciones* [MINAET]).

9. *Transitorio IV* of the Telecommunications Law.

10. *Ley de Fortalecimiento y Modernización de las Entidades Públicas del Sector Telecomunicaciones* (Law No. 8660, of August 13, 2008).

11. Created by Law 7593 of August 9, 1996.

12. Article 45 of ICE's law.

13. The initial members were appointed for three, four, and five years, with the intention of preserving the institutional memory of the entity while also delinking it from the electoral cycle (four years).

14. The law specifies this service as "circuit-switched," or "basic," service and limits this restriction to the executive, as it authorizes Congress to give basic service concessions.

15. The new procedures were intended to streamline the procurement process.

16. A subsidiary of Mexico's América Móvil operates with the commercial name Claro.

17. A subsidiary of Spain's Telefónica operates with the commercial name Movistar.

18. *Sala Constitucional de la Corte Suprema de Justicia ("Sala IV")*, Resolution No. 015763—2011 of November 16, 2011. The Court rejected an appeal from a citizen against a decision of the Municipality of Goicoechea to grant a permit for tower construction in that municipality, based, among other things, on the prevalence of public interest in the installation of telecommunications infrastructure over the entity's interest.

19. As reported during an interview with Victor Garcia, Director of Regulation for Claro, August 14, 2013.

20. In the case of Movistar, the information was reported during an interview with Juan Pablo Rivera, Director of Regulation, Telefónica de Costa Rica, August 13, 2013, as well as in the coverage map retrieved from http://www.telefonica.cr. In the case of Claro, the information was reported during an interview with Victor Garcia, Director of Regulation, Claro, August 14, 2013, as well as in the coverage map retrieved from http://www.claro.cr.

21. Costa Rica entered late into the provision of 3G services, while most other countries in Latin America had started offering 3G services in the early 2000s. 3G refers to third-generation systems, capable of providing voice and data communications at broadband speeds. 2G are digital systems for voice and low data rates, while 1G were analog systems.

22. The high value for Panama reveals that operators may not have removed inactive accounts from the database. This happens frequently as prepaid customers switch from one operator to another but leave the old line registered in the database. A value of more than 100 percent indicates that most inhabitants have a line, since some users have more than one.

23. It allows the user with an Internet connection to make telephone calls using services like Skype, Viber, and others.

24. ADSL uses the copper wires bandwidth above the voice to provide Internet access.

25. ICE introduced the iPhone on May 4, 2011 (Cordero Sancho 2011).

26. Cordero Perez (2008) citing results from the High-Tech Advisory Committee (*Comisión Asesora de Alta Tecnología* [CAATEC]) Barómetro CISCO results and quoting R. Monge.

27. ARESEP set the rates for prepaid service on March 31, 2008, by Resolution 8147-2008.

28. Telecommunications operators use many promotions, such as double minutes; buy a package and get 50 percent more minutes; reduced rates at non-peak traffic hours; call friends at lower rates; triple minutes on net; and others. Therefore, figure 4.12 may be misleading, because it does not include these promotions.

29. SUTEL Resolution 615-2009 of December 18, 2009, established that the ARESEP rates "temporarily" applied to all operators.

30. SUTEL, Resolution 295-2012 of October 3, 2012.

31. Again, comparisons depend on the plan chosen by the subscriber. Because of the variety of plans offered by each operator, the number of megabytes included in the rate, and the number of operators, it is difficult to compare rates across countries.

32. At the time of this writing, FONATEL had only four staff, including the director.

33. As reported by COMEX.

34. Buttkereit et al. (2009). A World Bank study found that every 10-percentage-point increase in broadband penetration accelerates economic growth by 1.38 percentage points for middle-income countries (Quiang, Rosotto, and Kimura 2009).

35. Quality refers to the fact that these frequencies are not in use by other operators.

36. Lower frequencies in the 700, 800, and 900 megahertz (MHz) bands offer four times the area of coverage for the same emitter power than high frequencies (1800, 1900, 2100, and 2500 MHz bands) and are useful for rural deployments, as fewer cell sites (towers) are needed to roll out the network.

37. The International Telecommunication Union approved the use of the 2,500–2,690 MHz band for mobile broadband; the band is called "IMT Extension" and was recommended at the World Radiocommunication Conference 2000.

38. A digital TV standard definition channel uses about one-fourth of the spectrum of an analog TV channel.

39. Agüero (2013) relates the case of Alta Vista Towers S.A. Costa Pacífico Torres Ltda. and Claro against the municipalities of Montes de Oca and Curridabat.

40. Articles 52 and 59 of the Telecommunications Law.

References

Agüero, M. 2013. "Tribunal condena a municipios por restricción a torres celulares." *La Nación*, August 20. http://www.nacion.com/nacional/Tribunal-condena-municipios-restriccion-celulares_0_1361063911.html.

Buttkereit, S., L. Enriquez, F. Grijpink, S. Moraje, W. Torfs, and T. Vaheri-Delmuelle. 2009. "Mobile Broadband for the Masses: Regulatory Levers to Make It Happen." http://www.mckinsey.com/client_service/telecommunications/latest_thinking/mobile_broadband_for_the_masses.

CISCO Barómetro. 2009. "VIII medición de la penetración de Internet de banda ancha en Costa Rica." http://www.caatec.org/sitio1/images/stories/publicaciones/barometro/barmetro-cisco-viii-informe-costa-rica-dic-2009.pdf.

Cordero Perez, C. 2008. "Costa Rica con Internet banda ancha mas caro." *El Financiero*, May 29.

———. 2009. "Apatia en ventas de 3G." *El Financiero*, December 20.

Cordero Sancho, M. 2011. "Apple domina en Costa Rica." *El Financiero*, September 1.

Kim, Y., T. Kelly, and S. Raja. 2010. *Building Broadband—Strategies and Policies for the Developing World*. Washington DC: World Bank.

MICITT (Ministerio de Ciencia, Tecnología y Telecomunicaciones). 2013. "A 5 años de la apertura de las telecomunicaciones en Costa Rica." Presentation made by RETEL at COMEX, San José, July.

ORBA (Observatorio Regional de Banda Ancha). 2012. *Estado de la banda ancha en Latinoamérica y el Caribe*. http://www.eclac.org/publicaciones/xml/9/48449 /EstadobandaAnchaenAMLC.pdf.

OECD (Organisation for Economic Co-operation and Development). 2009. "Broadband and the Economy." http://www.oecd.org/dataoecd/62/7/40781696.pdf.

Pineda, H. 2013. Presentation made during interview, San Jose, August 22.

Quiang, C., C. Rosotto, and K. Kimura. 2009. "Economic Impact of Broadband." In *Information and Communications for Development 2009: Extending Reach and Increasing Impact*, 35–50. Washington, DC: World Bank. http://issuu.com/world.bank .publications/docs/9780821376058.

SUTEL (Superintendencia de Telecomunicaciones). 2009. *Informe Técnico sobre el Uso y Asignación del Espectro Radioeléctrico en Costa Rica*. http://sutel.go.cr/.

———. 2010. *Modelo del Contrato: Plan de Desarrollo de la Red. Licitación Pública. Concesión para el Uso y Explotación del Espectro radioeléctrico para la Prestación de Servicios de Telecomunicaciones Móviles*. San José.

———. 2013. *Estadísticas del sector de telecomunicaciones*. Informe 2010–2012. San José.

CHAPTER 5

Intellectual Property Rights in CAFTA-DR and Pharmaceuticals in Costa Rica

Alejandra Castro

Introduction

Dominican Republic–Central America–United States Free Trade Agreement's (CAFTA-DR) chapter on the protection of intellectual property (IP) was controversial due to its potential implications for the pharmaceutical industry. The local generic industry argued that IP provisions would prevent the marketing approval of generic medicines and grant additional exclusive marketing rights by prohibiting drug regulatory agencies from using original pharmaceutical test data for the registration of generic medicines. This would have the effect of severely restricting or blocking generic competition. The strongest position against IP rules was that it would become economically unsustainable and legally impossible for the Costa Rican Social Security Administration (*Caja Costarricense de Seguro Social* [CCSS]), to provide universal coverage and access to medicines for the population, given that the prices of medicines were going to increase as a result of the agreement. Another group, however, believed that the IP provisions in CAFTA-DR would encourage innovative medicines to enter the market.

This chapter assesses the IP provisions within CAFTA-DR related to the pharmaceutical sector and whether those provisions have any effect on purchases of medicine by the CCSS. Even though it does not analyze the effect on prices resulting from the IP provisions, the analysis shows that CAFTA-DR includes provisions that allow access to low-cost pharmaceuticals. The number of medicines with some sort of IP protection is very small, including four pharmaceutical products (or two active ingredients) with patent linkages and 39 products (or 30 active ingredients) with protection of test data during 2009–12. Only one product with data protection has been added to the CCSS's Official Medicine List. Furthermore, the share of CCSS expenditures devoted to medicines has hovered around 8 percent during 2000–12, suggesting that IP provisions have not impacted medicine costs.

Intellectual Property Regulations for Pharmaceuticals in International Trade Treaties

Costa Rica's regulatory framework on IP for pharmaceuticals has been shaped by the Trade-Related Aspects of Intellectual Property Rights (TRIPS) and CAFTA-DR. Since 1996, Costa Rica is a signatory to the World Trade Organization (WTO) Agreement on TRIPS, which provided the baseline for IP protection for all WTO member countries. Costa Rica also adopted, along with all other WTO members, the 2001 Doha Declaration on TRIPS and Public Health, which clarified several TRIPS provisions on exemptions and exceptions contained in the agreement. For instance, it states that each member has the right to grant compulsory licenses and the freedom to determine the grounds upon which such licenses are granted. It also clarifies that each member country is free to establish its own regime of exhaustion of IP rights without challenge. When CAFTA-DR came into force in January 2009, it introduced additional regulations that affected IP provisions applicable to the pharmaceuticals market.

Several provisions in TRIPS and CAFTA-DR are related to pharmaceuticals, which guarantee that there is no real danger to Costa Rica's ability to access low-cost medicines. Based on these provisions, Costa Rica approved several regulations to ensure the implementation of agreements on IP and access to pharmaceuticals. For example, compulsory licensing exceptions, parallel importations, and the *Bolar* provision, which are not restricted by CAFTA-DR, are a significant guarantee of access to pharmaceuticals in line with international standards. The most relevant provisions in CAFTA-DR relate to patent protection systems, new chemical entities, the *Bolar* provision exception, patent term restoration, patent linkages, compulsory licensing, parallel importations, and data exclusivity. In particular, these provisions include the following:

- Patent protection systems.[1] Both TRIPS and CAFTA-DR required countries to create national patent protection regimes to issue patent licenses for inventions. The patent protection will last for 20 years from the date the patent application was filed. TRIPS defines what is considered an invention and details the kind of enforcement regime that countries must have, including civil and administrative procedures and remedies, provisional measures, border measures, and criminal procedures. CAFTA-DR does not prohibit the importation of pharmaceuticals via parallel importation.[2] Moreover, CAFTA-DR does not force countries to regulate second-use patents.[3]

- New chemical entity or new product.[4] CAFTA-DR defines a new chemical entity or new product by its novelty in the market in question. The implementation rules in Costa Rica limited the definition of new pharmaceutical products and new agricultural chemical entities, which resulted in excluding from this protection uses or indications, changes in the route of administration, dosage, dosage form or in the formulation of a chemical entity, as well as products that constitute combinations of chemical entities previously registered in the country. This definition includes a significant limitation on the number of drugs that could receive test data exclusivity protection in the country.

- Test data exclusivity.[5] One of the most controversial aspects of the present IP regulatory regime is the regulation of originator undisclosed information, including test data (that is, information that should be kept secret). CAFTA-DR confers nondisclosure rights of use for clinical information for a period of five years for pharmaceuticals and 10 years for agricultural chemicals after the product is approved in the country.[6] As a result, unless generic drug manufacturers generate this test data through their own means, they are forced to delay the marketing of the product, since without this information they cannot prove that the products are safe and effective.

- *Bolar* provision exception. By preserving the *Bolar* provision allowed under TRIPS,[7] CAFTA-DR gave generic medicine producers a victory. The *Bolar* provision in CAFTA-DR[8] is a limited exception to patent rights that enables companies to develop a generic product in order to obtain marketing approval and then enter the market as soon as the patent has expired. It sends a clear signal that third persons using IP material will be able to generate data for the creation of information that will be used to support market approval for a product (whether a pharmaceutical or agricultural chemical product).

- Patent term restoration. Under CAFTA-DR, the period of protection can be extended beyond 20 years if there have been delays in granting the patent license or analyzing the regulatory approval.[9] With the implementation rules, Costa Rica limited to a maximum of 18 months any extension of the duration of the patent protection to compensate for procedural delays (either in granting patents or in securing marketing approval for pharmaceuticals). The patent term restoration will apply in the following cases:
  - Delays of five years or more by the Industrial Property Registry from the date of filing of the patent,
  - Delays of three years or more by the Industrial Property Registry from the application of the substantive examination, or
  - Delays of three years or more by the Health Ministry in authorizing the commercialization of pharmaceutical products from the date of filing marketing approval of the drug product in the country.

- Patent linkages.[10] CAFTA-DR obliges regulatory authorities to prevent the registration and marketing of a generic product when the product has a patent. However, its implementation rules in Costa Rica do not allow the regulatory authority to reject a generic approval procedure based on patent linkage, and therefore the patent titleholder is forced to take further actions in court rather than in an administrative or regulatory level.

- Compulsory licensing.[11] One of the most important achievements of the CAFTA-DR negotiation in terms of patent protection and access to pharmaceuticals was in preserving the compulsory licensing provisions and exceptions under TRIPS as well as in those in regulations of the Costa Rican Patent Law. In order to obtain a compulsory license exception, the following must be analyzed:
  - If there have been unsuccessful attempts to obtain a voluntary license from the patent holder under reasonable terms and conditions and within a reasonable timeframe. This condition may be waived in the case of a national emergency.
  - If there are adequate payments made according to the circumstances appropriate for each case.
  - The decisions to apply this exception are subject to judicial review or another independent review by a superior and independent authority.

- Parallel imports. As under TRIPS, CAFTA-DR allows countries to determine their own rules on parallel imports, including from which market and at what price they will purchase pharmaceuticals. Parallel importation allows for the importation of a patented product that has been approved in a country's national market, as well as other markets abroad, but is sold for a lower price in other markets. Thus, parallel importations provide access to affordably priced medicines.

The provisions in TRIPS and CAFTA-DR could have affected producers of generic drugs in a narrow set of situations. One situation could have occurred if generic manufacturers were producing pharmaceuticals in violation of patents that have not expired. In this case, they would have contravened the protection of IP or the purchase regimes in place. Another situation could emerge as the generic manufacturers need to wait until the patent term has elapsed to sell their products. But this condition existed under TRIPS, before CAFTA-DR entered into effect. A third case is if the data protection for five years had required manufacturers to make reasonable efforts to invest in research and development to generate their own information to get a commercialization permit or wait until the five-year period expires. But, as indicated above, the implementation rules of CAFTA-DR limited the definition of new products and new chemical entities, so this situation has not occurred.

CAFTA-DR may also affect some innovative companies due to the limited definition of what is considered a new pharmaceutical product. This means that their rights to exercise exclusive dominion over their test data will be restricted when they register certain medicines. CAFTA-DR does not protect test data that have entered the public domain, nor does it protect test data that contain chemical entities that have already been registered (for example, a product that contains a combination of a new chemical product and one that was already registered would not classify for protection), even if the final product is innovative itself.

Data Protection, New Chemical Entities, and Patent Linkages after CAFTA-DR

One way to illustrate the impact of the clause on protection of test data and the narrow definition of new pharmaceutical products or chemical entities is to look at registrations for pharmaceutical products with the Ministry of Health. Only 30 active ingredients and 39 pharmaceutical specifications have received the protection of test data for five years in 2009–12 (see figure 5.1). This amounts to only 1 percent of the number of active ingredient registrations without test data protection during the same period. This is not surprising because most drugs developed every year and registered in the world by pharmaceutical companies are new presentations or formulations of preexisting medicine doses, rather than new drugs. In the case of the United States, for example, the Food and Drug Administration (FDA) approved 20 new molecular entities in 2005 and 35 in 2012.[12] Approximately two-thirds of the drugs approved by the FDA are not new molecular entities but amendments and new uses for existing drugs (Congressional Budget Office 2006).

Costa Rica has approved the registration of only four products (two active ingredients) at the Ministry of Health with patent linkage (see table 5.1). As mentioned in the previous section, patent linkage is a mechanism to promote effective and adequate IP protection. If a patent exists, marketing approval will not be granted to a generic version until the patent has expired or is found to be invalid. Patent linkage is a registered patent "linked" to the product that is covered by the patent in the market (Ferriter 2007).

Figure 5.1 Registration of Active Ingredients with the Ministry of Health in Costa Rica, 2003–12

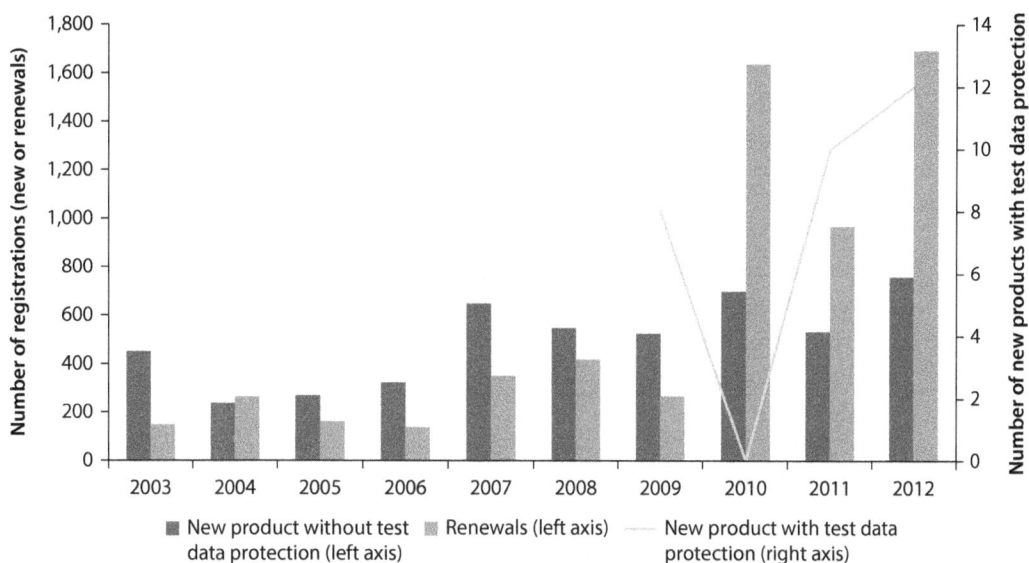

Source: Based on information provided by Laura Vargas Sanchez, Legal Counsel at the Health Products Directorate, Ministry of Health.

Table 5.1 Pharmaceutical Products with Patent Linkage Protection

Product name	Registry number	Registry date	Patent linkage number	Expiration date	Test data protection expiration date	Active ingredient
Champix 0.5 mg	4132-BM-5018	8/15/2007	2645	2/25/2020	8/15/2012	Vareniclina Tartrato
Champix 1 mg	4132-BM-5051	8/15/2007	2645	2/25/2020	8/15/2012	Vareniclina Tartrato
Celsentri 150 mg	4132-BM-3388	7/16/2008	2688	12/23/2018	7/16/2013	Maravoric
Celsentri 300 mg	4132-BM-3369	7/16/2008	2688	12/23/2018	7/16/2013	Maravoric

Source: Based on information reported by Costa Rica's Ministry of Health.

Figure 5.2 Costa Rica Patent Requests, 2000–12

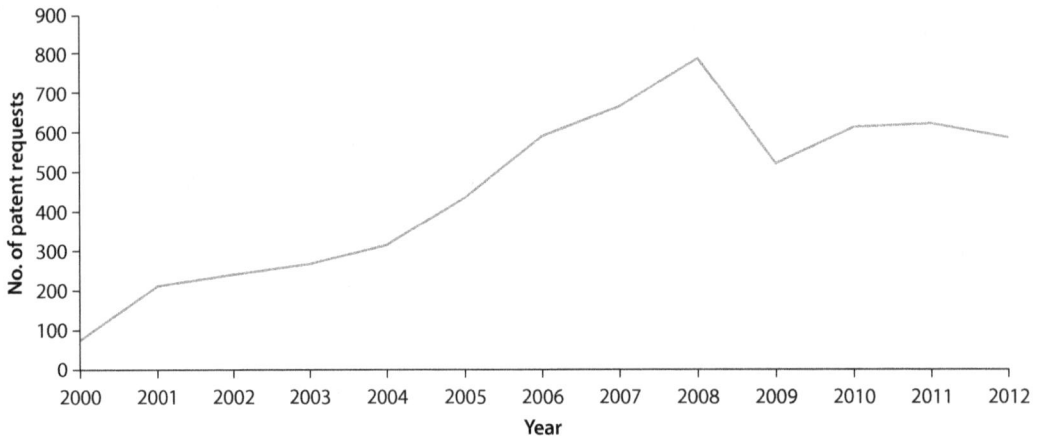

Source: Based on data provided by Luis Gustavo Alvarez, Director's Office, Industrial Property Registry.

Patent requests for all areas grew consistently until 2008, creating a potential backlog for reviews (see figure 5.2).[13] On average, about 590 new patent requests per year were submitted in 2009–12. Although data is not available on patent requests for pharmaceutical products, 2,410 innovations so far related to pharmaceutical, biotechnology, and chemical products are under analysis by the Patent Office to determine if they will receive patent protection or not. This is according to the Costa Rican National Intellectual Property Strategy of 2012 (Castro 2012), which included a complete study on pharmaceutical patents. However, it is well known that not all of these will pass the evaluation.

The number of patents issued has risen since 2008, but approvals are low compared to new patent requests. Most patents are issued for pharmaceutical products (see figure 5.3), which could be attributed to efforts by the Patent Office to avoid the implementation of the patent term restoration.

Figure 5.3 Costa Rica Patent Issues, 2000–12

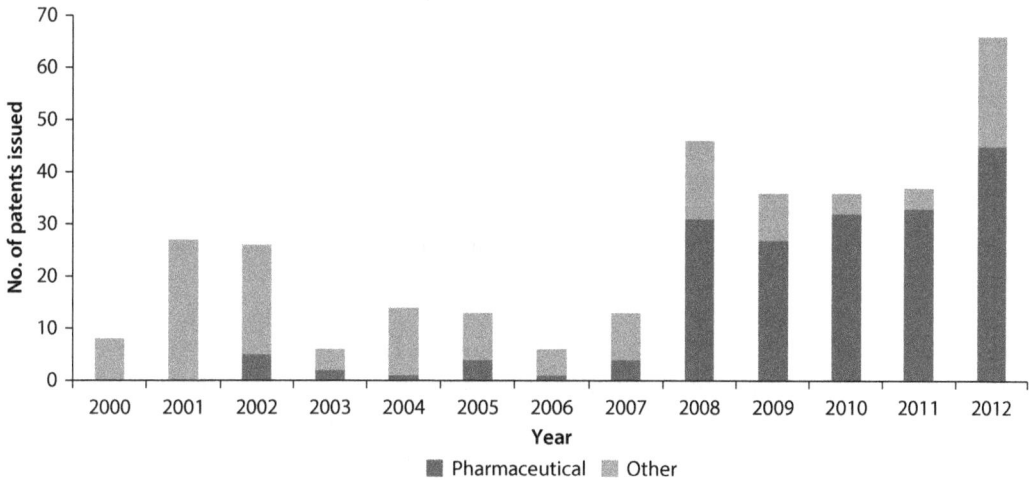

Source: Based on data provided by Luis Gustavo Alvarez, Director's Office, Industrial Property Registry.

How Have CAFTA-DR's IP Rules Affected the CCSS?

As the primary provider of Costa Rica's health care services, the CCSS has developed policies jointly with the Health Ministry to provide universal medicine coverage under human health rights regulations (CCSS and COMEX 2013). One of these policies is to define the essential medicine policy and the Official Medicine List, which includes those medicines deemed necessary to solve the majority of the population's health requirements. This list ensures that Costa Rica has access to the medications needed to treat the major causes of death and mortality affecting the population, and ensures that the medicines are available in the quantities and at the time that they are needed (CCSS and COMEX 2013). The purchase and supply of medicines for the national population is one of the most important activities of the CCSS, and it requires careful definition and management.

The definition of an essential medicine policy has three aspects (CCSS and COMEX 2013):

• Offer and medicine selection: Many chemical pharmaceutical entities exist for therapeutic and clinical uses, but not all of them are essential or necessary to address the country's health issues.
• Quality: The medicine that is going to be prescribed to the population must be safe and efficient.
• Sustainability of public health systems with limited budgets: The medicines to be considered must take into account international medicine market conditions and their costs.

Based on this definition, and following World Health Organization (WHO) recommendations, the CCSS published its essential medicine policy in 1985.[14] This policy has two basic components to ensure a rational use of medicines:

- Technical/scientific component: Medical management will conduct and be responsible for the selection, prescription, dispensation, and administration of the medicines, as well as for providing information and education about them.
- Operational component: Logistics management will be responsible for planning, acquisition, quality, storage, and distribution of the medicines.

A specific procedure regulates the inclusion of a medicine on the Official Medicine List, in accordance with several criteria. To add a new medicine or product to the list, there must be a demonstrated public health need. The analysis is made in accordance with epidemiological, clinical, pharmacological, and pharmacoeconomic criteria. Also, an analysis of available alternatives—including a review of scientific evidence, clinical trials, and meta-analysis—is needed to establish efficacy and safety (CCSS and COMEX 2013).

Since 1988, the Central Committee of Pharmacotherapy has been responsible for selecting medicines and keeping the Official Medicine List current. The Central Committee of Pharmacotherapy is a scientific and technical body established in 1982 by the CCSS.[15] The committee includes 13 national hospital specialist doctors and three pharmacists. Its main objective is to ensure the population's access to medicine and the rational use of those medicines. Once committee requirements have been met, they can add to the Official Medicine List, which can be found on the CCSS webpage.[16]

The CCSS Official Medicine List is continuously updated as new medicines are evaluated. Currently, the list includes 455 active ingredients in 641 pharmaceutical presentations and 36 active ingredients not registered before the Ministry of Health, which have been selected and included on the list according to the procedure indicated above (CCSS and COMEX 2013). The drugs included on the list do not constitute the totality of the medicines on the Costa Rican market, but only the medications that the central committee considers necessary to address the population's health issues. Between January 2009 and May 2013, the list was updated with seven new active ingredients and 12 pharmaceutical presentations.

Pharmaceutical innovation drives constant change in the medical field and has a significant impact on the CCSS's list. The challenge is to define how many and which of the new medicines introduced to the market really represent actual progress. Between 2001 and 2010, only 2 percent of medicines that entered the market were a real advance to medicine, 14 percent were not acceptable, 7 percent could offer some advantage over available treatment options, 21 percent could offer some help, 52 percent did not represent any significant advantage, and 5 percent showed inconclusive results (Gagnon 2012).

The CCSS purchase policy for medicine allows the institution to make a careful selection of the medicines required to address public health problems.

The purchase policy avoids the duplication of products used for specific diseases, which in turn creates an environment for more competitive pricing. This policy allows for stability in the Official Medicine List. For the last four years, the CCSS has added only 1.6 active ingredients per year on average. The implementation of the policy has also demonstrated that not all drugs on the market that are considered necessary for public health care need to be incorporated into the CCSS Official Medicine List. In fact, out of the total number of chemical-pharmaceutical entities in the world, only 4.91 percent are included in the CCSS Official Medicine List to address the public health problems of the national population.

For some of the new products included in the CCSS Official Medicine List since 2009, no generic medicines are registered in Costa Rica. Therefore, access to generics is not related to the protection of IP, because even when new products do not have data exclusivity or any other IP right, they do not have a generic version in the market. Such is the case for three vaccines, for Gadoversetamide (gadoteric acid), and for Levobupivacaine. The reasons for this situation are varied. In some cases, the manufacturing complexity or low profitability of the drug removes incentives for generic pharmaceutical companies to produce the generic version. Most of them even wait until a medicine is included on the Official Medicine List before producing the drug as a generic to ensure that there will be an attractive market.

Costa Rican law grants the government sufficient power to adopt all the necessary steps to assure that the patent process of medicines will not affect its availability to the population. The implementation of CAFTA-DR did not change the patent process, nor does it prohibit generic medicine production, marketing, importation, purchase, or distribution. The treaty simply establishes five years of protection for all the generated test data in order to protect information on the new medicine's safety and efficacy, in accordance with worldwide protection standards. However, this information is not exclusive and therefore the protection is for nondisclosure purposes. On data protection of new pharmaceutical products, CAFTA-DR does not prohibit the production, commercialization, importation, purchase, or distribution of generic medicines.

To analyze the impact of CAFTA-DR's data protection rules on the CCSS Official Medicine List, a review of the list and registered pharmaceutical products over the last four years is needed. Between CAFTA-DR's entry into force and May 2013, only seven active ingredients and 12 pharmaceutical presentations have been added to the CCSS Official Medicine List, approximately 1.6 active ingredients and 2.7 pharmaceutical presentations per year. The newly introduced medicine with data protection was Tenofovir disoproxil fumarate (Viread 300 mg tablets), for which data protection will expire in May 2016.

During the first four years of CAFTA-DR enforcement in Costa Rica, data protection and patent linkages were not the determining factors for the inclusion of a product on the CCSS Official Medicine List. The inclusion of a medicine on the Official Medicine List was not impacted by the CAFTA-DR's rules on data protection or patent linkages, but rather by other considerations, including price, production technology, economic viability of generic medicine pharmaceutical manufacturers, and the complexity and quality of the products required by the CCSS. These factors have not been modified after CAFTA-DR's entry into force. Only one product with data protection has been included on the CCSS Official Medicine List (Tenofovir disoproxil fumarate). The Official Medicine List does not include any of the four products with patent linkages in Costa Rica (see table 5.1 for the list of products), and thus the CCSS does not buy them.

Given that very few of the medicines in the official list have either data protections or patent linkages, these rules have not impacted the CCSS. As discussed above, the CCSS includes medicines on its Official Medicine List based on the population's health needs and not according to any IP requirements. In addition, it is not necessary for a medicine to have patent linkage to be included on the Official Medicine List. The only products that have patent linkage in Costa Rica were not included on the CCSS Official Medicine List since the Central Committee of Pharmacotherapy does not consider them necessary to treat diseases or ensure public health.

Expenditure growth at CCSS cannot be attributed to an increase in the prices for medicines. CCSS expenditure on medicines amounted to US$204 million in 2012, accounting for 8 percent of total CCSS expenditure (see figure 5.4). This share dropped from a peak of 10 percent in 2007, suggesting that factors besides medicines are affecting CCSS expenditure. A recent study by the Pan American Health Organization (PAHO) shows that one of the main determinants of the difficult financial situation of CCSS is the high level of staff remunerations (salaries and social security contributions) (PAHO 2011). That study also shows that the share of staff remunerations as a percent of total health care expenditure

Figure 5.4 CCSS Expenditures for Health Care and Medicine

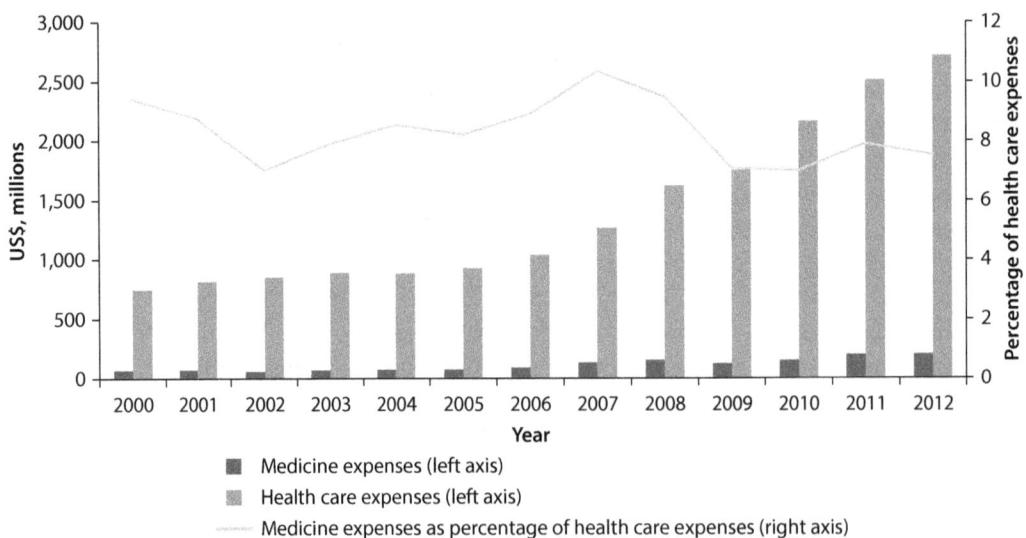

Medicine expenses (left axis)
Health care expenses (left axis)
Medicine expenses as percentage of health care expenses (right axis)

Source: Based on data provided by the Costa Rican Social Security Administration (*Caja Costarricense de Seguro Social* [CCSS]).

increased from 54.0 percent in 2000 to 68.5 percent in 2010, illustrating that those expenses have been growing faster than other expenditure categories, including purchase of medicines.

When examining medicine expenses, a small group of medicines account for half of the expenditures. Antineoplastic products, which are used to treat cancer, increased to 37 percent of medicine purchases in 2012, from 11 percent in 2007 (see figure 5.5). During the same period, the share of biologics and vaccines increased to 6 percent.

Increasing investment in innovative products has been largely attributed to production costs rather than IP protection. In the past several years, in particular in 2009, investment in innovative products increased as a result of the entry of biological and biotechnological medicines in Costa Rica (CCSS and COMEX 2013). This situation has arisen due to the cost of production for these kinds of medicines, rather than to IP protection.[17]

When examining CCSS investments in medicines by type, some interesting trends emerged. First, the gap between CCSS investments in national and foreign generic medicines has grown since 2009 (see figure 5.6). Furthermore, investments in innovative and biologic/biotechnology medicines are also growing. It is not possible to determine from the data whether CCSS purchases in medicines have shifted from national to foreign markets.

In summary, the IP provisions with CAFTA-DR did not diminish the country's ability to get medicines to ensure the health of the Costa Rican population. The decision to add medicines to the CCSS Official Medicine List depends on specific procedures regarding its efficacy and safety rather than with the IP provisions in CAFTA-DR.

Figure 5.5 Percentage Distribution of CCSS Medicine Expenditures by Therapeutic Group, 2007–12

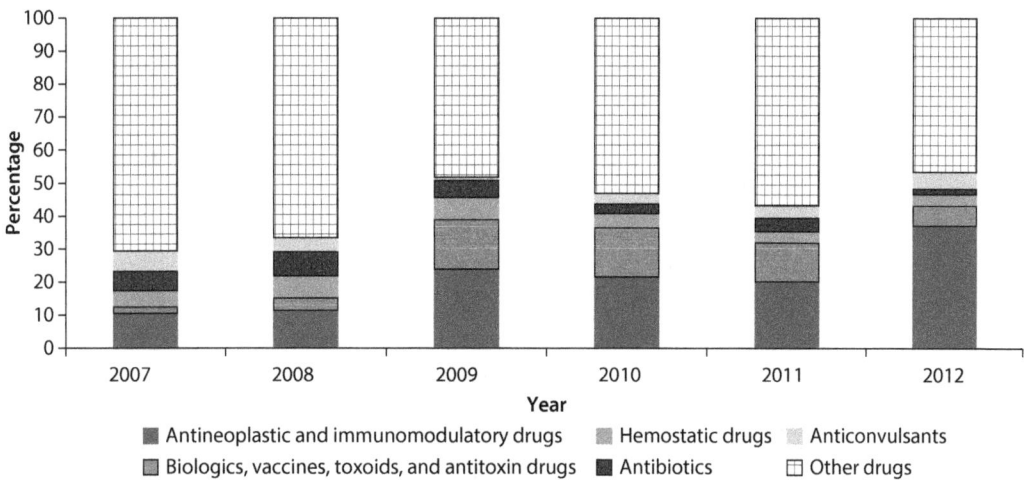

Legend:
■ Antineoplastic and immunomodulatory drugs   ■ Hemostatic drugs   ▨ Anticonvulsants
■ Biologics, vaccines, toxoids, and antitoxin drugs   ■ Antibiotics   ▦ Other drugs

Source: Based on data provided by the Costa Rican Social Security Administration (*Caja Costarricense de Seguro Social* [CCSS]).
Note: The data includes only medicine purchases made at the central level, which ranges between 81–89 percent of total medicine purchases by CCSS. Purchases made by executing units (*unidades ejecutoras de las unidades de atención*) were excluded.

Figure 5.6 CCSS Medicine Purchases by Type, 2003–12

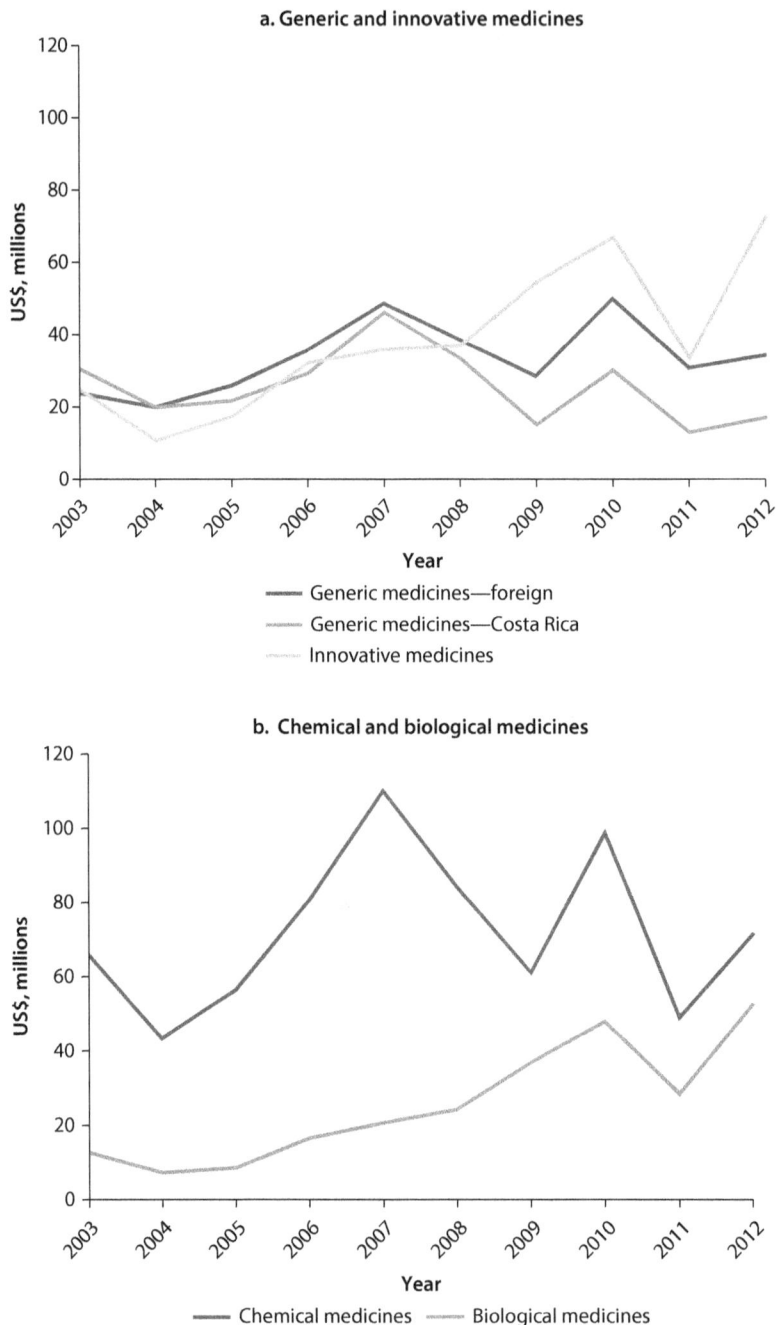

a. Generic and innovative medicines

US$, millions

Year

—— Generic medicines—foreign
—— Generic medicines—Costa Rica
—— Innovative medicines

b. Chemical and biological medicines

US$, millions

Year

—— Chemical medicines   —— Biological medicines

Source: Based on data provided by the Costa Rican Social Security Administration (*Caja Costarricense de Seguro Social* [CCSS]).
Note: The data only include medicine purchases made at the central level, which ranges between 81 and 89 percent of total medicine purchase. Purchases made by executing units (*unidades ejecutoras de las unidades de atención*) were excluded.

Notes

1. Patents provide the patent owner with the legal means to prevent others from making, using, or selling the new invention for a limited period of time (20 years), subject to a number of exceptions.

2. Parallel importation allows for the importation of a patented product that has been approved in a country's national market, as well as other markets abroad, but is sold for a lower price in another country. This is an important provision to ensure access to affordably priced medicines. Article 6 of TRIPS allows countries to determine their own rules on parallel importation.

3. Second-use patents—whether a result of a new registration or of new associated claims (the discovery of new uses)—are not recognized in Costa Rica.

4. Article 8 of the Costa Rican Undisclosed Information Law states that: "A new product" means one that does not contain a chemical entity that has been previously approved in Costa Rica. Executive Decree No. 34927-J-COMEX-S-MAG, Undisclosed Information Law Regulations in Article 4, defines it as "a pharmaceutical product that does not contain a chemical entity in the product formula that already has a regulatory approval in Costa Rica. It will not be considered a new chemical entity if those entities include new uses or indications, changes in the administration route, dosage, dosage form or formulation of a chemical entity, or those products constituting combinations of chemical entities previously registered in the country."

5. Test data is defined as the clinical information generated by companies that have investment in research and development of new chemical and agro-chemical entities, with the purpose of demonstrating the new entities' efficacy and safety.

6. See Article 15.10 of CAFTA-DR.

7. See Article 30 of TRIPS.

8. See Article 15.9.5 of CAFTA-DR.

9. See Article 15.9.6 of CAFTA-DR.

10. Patent linkage refers to a system where drugs covered by a patent are linked before the regulatory authority with the patent, for patent enforcement purposes, to prevent generic approval to sell the drug.

11. Through compulsory licensing, a government temporarily overrides a patent in the public interest and negotiates a better price for the medication or seeks the approval for licensing for production of generic versions of a patent product, which are generally at a lower cost.

12. See Congressional Budget Office (2006) for 2005 data and Food and Drug Administration (2012) for 2012 data.

13. The list of registered products is available at: http://www.ministeriodesalud.go.cr /index.php/informacion/productos-registrados?start=8.

14. The essential medicine policy was established by the Executive Decree No. 19343-S, December 19, 1989. Article 16 of the Decree states: "Public Health Institutions must have a basic form of medicine with the corresponding administrative regulations and therapeutic information, in accordance with the National Therapeutic Formulary. For this purpose and to ensure the correct application of this Regulation, each institution will establish a Pharmacotherapy Committee, which will also be responsible for approving the purchase of pharmaceutical products that are not included in the National Therapeutic Formulary in cases of exceptional urgency and necessity. In any

case, this determination must be made known to the Committee with information and data necessary to justify such a decision."

15. See the Executive Decree No. 13878-SPPS, September 22, 1982.

16. See http://www.ccss.sa.cr/medicamentos.

17. Information obtained from CCSS Budget Direction.

References

CCSS (Caja Costarricense de Seguro Social) and COMEX (Ministerio de Comercio Exterior). 2013. Análisis del impacto del tratado de libre comercio entre República Dominicana, Centroamérica y Estados Unidos: A sus cuatro años de vigencia en la Caja Costarricense de Seguro Social. Unpublished document.

Castro, A. 2012. *Estrategia nacional de propiedad intelectual*. Document prepared for the Ministry of Justice in Costa Rica in cooperation with Organización mundial de la propiedad intelectual (OMPI) and under the supervision of Comisión Interinstitucional de Propiedad Intelectual (CIPPI). http://www.micit.go.cr/index.php/component /content/article/1142.html.

Congressional Budget Office. 2006. *Research and Development in the Pharmaceutical Industry*. Washington, DC: Congressional Budget Office. http://www.cbo.gov/sites /default/files/cbofiles/ftpdocs/76xx/doc7615/10-02-drugr-d.pdf.

Ferriter, K. L. 2007. "Linkages between Generic Approval and the Patent System in the United States." Powerpoint slides. http://www.stockholm-network.org/downloads /events/Linkages_Between_Generic_Approval_and_the_Patent_System_in_the_US _Karin_Ferriter_USPTO.pdf.

Food and Drug Administration. 2012. *FY12 Innovative Drug Approvals: Bringing Life-Saving Drugs to Patients Quickly and Efficiently*. Washington, DC: Food and Drug Administration. http://www.fda.gov/downloads/aboutfda/reportsmanualsforms /reports/ucm330859.pdf.

Gagnon, M. A. 2012. "Pooling of All Prescrire's Data Collected Since 1981." *Prescrire* 32 (342): 311–14.

PAHO (Pan American Health Organization). 2011. *Informe sobre el estado de situacion financiera del seguro de salud de la Caja Costarricense del Seguro Social*. Washington, DC: PAHO.

Legal Changes under CAFTA-DR

The table below includes a list of all the legislation that Costa Rica produced to implement its obligation under CAFTA-DR and achieved its entry into force on January 1, 2009. This legislative implementation consisted of the promulgation of more than 10 laws, including the ratification of 3 international treaties, and about 30 executive decrees and resolutions.[1]

Table A.1 Legal Changes under CAFTA-DR

Subject	Implementation of legislation
National treatment and market access for goods	Executive Decree No. 34912-COMEX of November 25, 2008, "Reglamento para la distribución y asignación de contingentes arancelarios de importación otorgados al amparo del Tratado de libre comercio República Dominicana, Centroamérica y Estados Unidos."
	Executive Decree No. 34926-COMEX of November 27, 2008, "Contingentes arancelarios de importación de arroz en granza otorgados al amparo del Tratado de libre comercio República Dominicana, Centroamérica y Estados Unidos y 34926-COMEX."
	Executive Decree No. 36598-COMEX of February 23, 2011, that established a Committee on Agricultural Trade.
Rules of origin and origin procedures	Executive Decree No. 34753-H-COMEX of September 16, 2008, "Reglamento para la aplicación y administración de las disposiciones aduaneras y de las reglas de origen del CAFTA-DR."
Commercial defense	Executive Decree No. 34755-COMEX-MEIC of August 22, 2008, "Implementación de la Sección A: Salvaguardias del Capítulo Ocho Defensa Comercial, del Tratado de Libre Comercio República Dominicana-Centroamérica-Estados Unidos."
Government procurement	Law No. 8630 of January 17, 2008, that modified the Criminal Code (Law No. 4573) and the Law Against Corruption and Illicit Proceeds (Law No. 8422).
Cross-border trade in services	Law No. 8629 of November 30, 2007, "Modificación de la Ley de Protección al Representante de Casas Extranjeras No. 6209, and Repeal of subsection b) of article 361 of the Commercial Code, Law No. 3284."
Financial services	Approved resolution by article 28 of the meeting No. 569-2006 that took place on April 6, 2006, of CONASSIF "Reglamentación general para las empresas responsables de la administración de los fondos de inversión en Costa Rica."
	SUPEN Resolution of November 6, 2006, "Regulación SP-A-036 relativa a fondos de pensiones y fondos de pensiones complementarias."

table continues next page

Table A.1 Legal Changes under CAFTA-DR *(continued)*

Subject	Implementation of legislation
Insurance	Law No. 8653 of July 22, 2008, "Ley Reguladora del Mercado de Seguros," which includes reforms to Law No. 12 of October 30, 1924, and establishes rules to regulate the opening of the insurance market.
	Executive Decree No. 34924-MP-H-COMEX of November 26, 2008, "Garantía Estatal a favor del Instituto Nacional de Seguros."
	Approved resolution by article 7 of the meeting No. 744-1-008 of CONASSIF "Reglamento sobre la Solvencia de Entidades de Seguros y Reaseguros."
	Approved resolution by article 6 of the meeting No. 744-2008 of CONASSIF "Reglamento sobre Autorizaciones, Registros y Requisitos de Funcionamiento de Entidades Supervisadas por la Superintendencia General de Seguros."
	Law No. 8642 of June 4, 2008, "Ley General de Telecomunicaciones," establishes rules to regulate the opening of the telecommunications market following the CAFTA-DR guidelines.
Telecommunications	Law No. 8660 of August 2008, "Ley de Fortalecimiento y Modernización de las Entidades Públicas del Sector de Telecomunicaciones," that establishes a legal framework for the strengthening of ICE.
	Executive Decree No. 34765-MINAET, "Reglamento a la Ley General de Telecomunicaciones" of September 22, 2008, and its modifications: Executive Decree No. 34916-MINAET, "Modificación al Reglamento a la Ley General de Telecomunicaciones of December 1, 2008."
	Resolution of the Board of Directors of the ARESEP of October 6, 2008, "Reglamento de Acceso e Interconexión de Redes de Telecomunicaciones."
	Resolution of the Board of Directors of the ARESEP of October 6, 2008, "Reglamento de Acceso Universal, Servicio Universal y Solidaridad."
	Resolution of the Board of Directors of the ARESEP of October 6, 2008, "Reglamento del Régimen de Competencia en Telecomunicaciones."
	Law No. 8631 of March 6, 2008, "Ley de protección de las obtenciones vegetales."
Intellectual property rights	Law No. 8632 of March 28, 2008, "Modificación de varios artículos de la ley de marcas y otros signos distintivos, ley N° 7978, de la ley de patentes de invención, dibujos y modelos industriales y modelos de utilidad N° 6867 y de la ley de la biodiversidad N° 7788."
	Law No. 8633 of April 4, 2008, "Adhesión de Costa Rica al Tratado de Budapest sobre el reconocimiento internacional del depósito de micro organismos a los fines del procedimiento en materia de patentes."
	Law No. 8834 of May 3, 2008, "Reforma del artículo 2 de la ley N° 6683, de 14 de octubre de 1982, y el artículo 52 de la ley N° 8039, de 12 de octubre de 2000."
	Law No. 8635 of April 21, 2008, "Aprobación del Convenio Internacional para la Protección de las Obtenciones Vegetales."
	Law No. 8636 of April 29, 2008, "Ley de Aprobación de la Adhesión de Costa Rica al Tratado sobre el derecho de marcas y su Reglamento."
	Law No. 8656 of July 18, 2008, "Modificación de varios artículos de la Ley de Procedimientos de Observancia de los Derechos de Propiedad Intelectual N° 8039."
	Law No. 8686 of November 21, 2008, "Reforma, Adición y Derogación de varias normas que regulan materias relacionadas con Propiedad Intelectual."
	Executive Decree No. 34756-J-COMEX, of September 17, 2008, "Reforma al artículo 21 del Reglamento de las Disposiciones Relativas a las Indicaciones Geográficas y Denominaciones de Origen, contenidas en la Ley de Marcas y Otros Signos Distintivos, Ley N° 7978."
	Executive Decree No. 34760-J-COMEX, of September 18, 2008, "Reforma al artículo 22 del Reglamento de la Ley de Marcas y otros signos Distintivos, Decreto Ejecutivo N° 32033-J del 20 de febrero de 2002."

table continues next page

Table A.1 Legal Changes under CAFTA-DR *(continued)*

Subject	Implementation of legislation
Intellectual property rights	Executive Decree No. 34904-J of November 21, 2008, "Modificaciones al Reglamento a la Ley de Derechos de Autor y Derechos Conexos."
	Executive Decree No. 34758-J-COMEX of September 18, 2008, "Modificaciones al Reglamento de la Ley de Patentes de Invención, Dibujos y Modelos Industriales y Modelos de Utilidad, Decreto Ejecutivo N° 15222-MIEM-J del 12 de diciembre de 1983."
	Executive Decree No. 34925-S-COMEX of November 27, 2008, "Modificación al Reglamento de Inscripción, Control, Importación y Publicidad de Medicamentos."
	Executive Decree No. 34903-MAG-S-MINAET-MEIC-COMEX of November 21, 2008. By the Executive Decree No. 35828-MAG-S-MINAET-MEIC-COMEX of February 25, 2010, "La Derogación, adición y modificaciones de determinadas disposiciones relativas al Reglamento sobre el Registro, Uso y Control de Plaguicidas Sintéticos Formulados, Ingrediente Activo Grado Técnico, Coadyuvantes y Sustancias Afines de Uso Agrícola."
	Executive Decree No. 34927-J-COMEX-S-MAG, of November 28, 2008, "Reglamento a la Ley de Información No Divulgada."
	Executive Decree No. 36880-COMEX-JP of October 18, 2011, "Reglamento sobre la limitación a la responsabilidad de los proveedores de servicios por infracciones a Derechos de Autor y Conexos de Acuerdo con el Artículo 15.11.27 del Tratado de Libre Comercio República Dominicana-Centroamérica- Estados Unidos."
	Executive Decree No. 34757-MTSS-COMEX of September 19, 2008, "Implementación del Capítulo 16 Laboral del Tratado de Libre Comercio República Dominicana-Centroamérica-Estados Unidos, Ley de aprobación N° 8622 del 21 de noviembre de 2007."
Labor	Executive Decree No. 34754–MINAET-COMEX of September 17, 2008, "Implementación del Capítulo 17 Ambiental del Tratado de Libre Comercio República Dominicana-Centroamérica-Estados Unidos."
Environment	Executive Decree No. 34958-MINAET-COMEX of December 11, 2008, "Reglamento al Artículo 80 de la Ley de Biodiversidad, Ley N° 7788 del 30 de abril de 1998."
	Executive Decree No. 34959-MINAET-COMEX of December 11, 2008, "Reglamento al Artículo 78, Inciso 6) de la Ley de Biodiversidad, Ley N° 7788 del 30 de abril de 1998."
Transparency	Law No. 8630 of January 17, 2008, modified the Criminal Code (Law No. 4573) and the Law Against Corruption and Illicit Proceeds (Law No. 8422).

Source: Information provided by COMEX (the Ministry of Foreign Trade [*Ministerio de Comercio Exterior*]), with inputs from Eric Scharf.

Note

1. The objectives of this legislative implementation are to ensure the correct application of the treaty and to maximize its potential for Costa Rica.

Costa Rica's Trade Partners

Table B.1 Stylized Facts on Regional Trade Patterns

Export as percentage of total (FOB)		1980	1990	2000	2010	2012
Costa Rica	to Central America	21	21	14	14	32
	to United States	39	38	55	46	34
	to rest of the world	40	41	31	40	34
Dominican Republic	to Central America	4	2	1	0.1	0.2
	to United States	53	57	87	67	46
	to rest of the world	43	41	12	33	53
El Salvador	to Central America	42	40	27	32	29
	to United States	47	49	66	34	42
	to rest of the world	12	12	7	34	29
Guatemala	to Central America	32	33	33	28	31
	to United States	40	39	36	41	29
	to rest of the world	28	28	30	31	40
Honduras	to Central America	21	24	24	4	12
	to United States	35	37	57	63	53
	to rest of the world	45	39	19	33	35
Nicaragua	to Central America	11	12	28	15	20
	to United States	56	53	42	11	39
	to rest of the world	33	35	30	74	42
Panama	to Central America	13	15	17	13	16
	to United States	21	30	49	46	58
	to rest of the world	66	55	34	41	26
Imports as percentage of total (CIF)		1980	1990	2000	2010	2012
Costa Rica	from Central America	8	7	9	9	17
	from United States	51	47	36	41	34
	from rest of the world	42	46	55	50	49
Dominican Republic	from Central America	3	4	3	1.9	1.5
	from United States	40	41	61	41	45
	from rest of the world	57	55	37	57	54

table continues next page

Table B.1 Stylized Facts on Regional Trade Patterns *(continued)*

Imports as percentage of total (CIF)		1980	1990	2000	2010	2012
El Salvador	from Central America	22	23	20	18	35
	from United States	38	37	52	44	20
	from rest of the world	40	41	29	38	45
Guatemala	from Central America	14	14	15	9	14
	from United States	38	37	41	40	35
	from rest of the world	47	48	44	52	51
Honduras	from Central America	24	19	24	9	11
	from United States	44	41	48	44	42
	from rest of the world	32	41	28	47	46
Nicaragua	from Central America	26	27	29	19	36
	from United States	19	24	28	15	28
	from rest of the world	55	49	43	66	37
Panama	from Central America	11	11	8	6	5
	from United States	34	38	38	43	37
	from rest of the world	54	50	55	51	58

Source: Based on data from Direction of Trade Statistics, International Monetary Fund.
Note: CIF = cost, insurance, and freight; FOB = free on board.

Gravity Model

Introduction and Literature

Models called gravity models are extensively used in trade literature to explain econometrically the ex post effects of economic integration agreements on trade flows. The "gravity model" name is derived from its resemblance to Newton's law of gravity, and in it trade flows between countries are described as an economic function of their incomes or "sizes," physical distances between them, and trade barriers, among others. The studies of Anderson (1979) and Bergstrand (1985) provided early formal theoretical foundations for the gravity equation based on utility and profit maximization. Given the solid microeconomic foundations underlining the general model, the gravity model is among the most comprehensive models used in the trade literature.

An empirical application of Bergstrand's theoretical foundation of the gravity model was used by Gould (1998) to determine the effects on trade flows of the North American Free Trade Agreement (NAFTA) between the United States, Canada, and Mexico. Gould used a bilateral approach to the gravity model and estimated the effects of NAFTA on exports and imports between the United States and Canada, the United States and Mexico, and Canada and Mexico, separately.

Following Gould (1998), the current study applies the gravity model to a case of bilateral trade flows between Costa Rica and the United States using a time series sample in order to determine the effects of CAFTA-DR on exports from Costa Rica to the United States and imports from the United States to Costa Rica. As the physical distance between Costa Rica and the United States does not vary over time, the measure of "distance" is not included in the underlying model for this study.

Within the Costa Rica context, the study of Jaramillo and Lederman (2006) provided a preliminary assessment of the expected trade and nontrade benefits of CAFTA-DR in the moment it was signed in 2004 and while it was being negotiated. Their study, drawing from different approaches and methodologies, concluded that CAFTA-DR was likely to generate greater trade levels arising from the removal of most tariff and quota barriers among all the parties involved in the agreement. This in turn would improve growth levels.

Four years after the ratification of the CAFTA-DR in Costa Rica in 2009, the present study provides some empirical evidence of the effects of the free trade agreement on Costa Rican trade flows. This evidence corroborates, to a certain extent, the assessment of the potential trade benefits found in Jaramillo and Lederman (2006). Furthermore, the study provides a simple but comprehensive framework to evaluate the increases in trade flows that occurred due to the CAFTA-DR and evaluate their magnitude and importance.

The findings of this study have to be read with caution and can only be seen as an indication of a link between CAFTA-DR and trade flows. The reasons are difficulties in identifying and disentangling the effects from CAFTA-DR and earlier trade agreements as well as simultaneous events such as the global financial and economic crisis.

Data

The data to be used in the gravity model are quarterly data for the 1997–2013 period. For trade flows the value (in millions of USD) of exports and imports of goods between Costa Rica and the United States is used as provided by the Central Bank of Costa Rica. As discussed, the gravity model includes the size of the economy; the most comprehensive measure to account for this is real gross domestic product (GDP) of Costa Rica (1991 colones, millions) and the real GDP of the United States (2009 US$, billions). In order to control for prices, the GDP price deflator for Costa Rica and the United States is used. In order to control for Costa Rica's external conditions with the United States and the rest of the world, the real effective exchange rates between Costa Rica and the United States and between Costa Rica and the rest of the world (excluding the United States), respectively, are used.[1]

Model

To assess the effects of CAFTA-DR since its signing, the following benchmark gravity model of Costa Rican and U.S. bilateral trade flows is estimated using quarterly data from 1997 through 2013 (first quarter). The empirical equations are based on the application of the gravity model found in Gould (1988), which is derived from standard microeconomic foundations of Bergstrand (1985). All variables are seasonally adjusted quarterly data and are expressed in log first-differences (growth rates):

$$X_t^{ij} = \alpha_0 + \alpha_1 X_{t-q_1}^{ij} + \alpha_2 GDP_{t-q_2}^{i} + \alpha_3 GDP_{t-q_3}^{j} + \alpha_4 P_{t-q_4}^{i} + \alpha_5 P_{t-q_5}^{j}$$
$$+ \alpha_6 E_{t-q_6}^{ij} + \alpha_7 E_{t-q_7}^{iw} + \alpha_8 D_t + \alpha_9 CAFTA_t + \varepsilon_t \tag{1}$$

$$M_t^{ij} = \beta_0 + \beta_1 M_{t-p_1}^{ij} + \beta_2 GDP_{t-p_2}^{i} + \beta_3 GDP_{t-p_3}^{j} + \beta_4 P_{t-p_4}^{i} + \beta_5 P_{t-p_5}^{j}$$
$$+ \beta_6 E_{t-p_6}^{ij} + \beta_7 E_{t-p_7}^{iw} + \beta_8 D_t + \beta_9 CAFTA_t + \mu_t \tag{2}$$

The variables are defined as follows: X^{ij} is country i's (Costa Rica) exports to country j (United States); t refers to the quarterly date; q_n (where n=1,2,...,7) refers to the number of periods each individual independent variable in equation (1) is lagged[2]; p_n (where n=1,2,...,7) refers to the number of periods each individual independent variable in equation (2) is lagged[3]; M^{ij} is country i's (Costa Rica) imports from country j (United States); GDP^i is real gross domestic product of country i and GDP^j is real gross domestic product of country j; P^i is the GDP price deflator of country i and P^j is the GDP price deflator of country j; E^{ij} is the real effective exchange rate between country i and country j, and E^{iw} is the real effective exchange rate between country i and the rest of the world (excluding country j). D_t represents other free trade agreements signed by Costa Rica during the period 1997–2013. *CAFTA* is a binary variable representing the period in which CAFTA-DR was signed[4] in Costa Rica (August 5, 2004). *CAFTA* equals 1 beginning the third quarter of 2004 and 0 before that.

Three different regressions were estimated for both the equation on exports (1) and imports (2). These three different regressions include different dummies for CAFTA-DR: (a) CAFTA starting in 2004 ($CAFTA_{04}$); (b) two different CAFTA-DR dummies for when it was signed in 2004 and for its ratification in 2009 ($CAFTA_{04}$ and $CAFTA_{09}$, respectively); and (c) only CAFTA-DR when it was ratified ($CAFTA_{09}$). The size and statistical significance of the CAFTA coefficients tell us the degree to which CAFTA-DR affects bilateral trade flows in Costa Rica.

Methodology and Results

The Box-Jenkins methodology was used in order to determine the lag structure and select the model's underlying equations (1) and (2). This methodology, after identifying the variables' stationarity and correcting for seasonality, consists of using plots for autocorrelation and partial autocorrelation to decide which autoregressive components and lags of the independent variable should be used in the model. The results of the model selection for equations (1) and (2) using the Box-Jenkins methodology are presented below:

$$\text{Equation (1): } q_1 = 1, q_2 = 4, q_3 = 1, q_4 = 1, q_5 = 1, q_6 = 1, q_7 = 1$$

$$\text{Equation (2): } p_1 = 4, p_2 = 2, p_3 = 3, p_4 = 2, p_5 = 1, p_6 = 4, p_7 = 4$$

Once the lag structure is determined for models (1) and (2), they are estimated by ordinary least squares (OLS). The results are presented in tables C.1 and C.2.

Having estimated the sign and magnitude of the effects of CAFTA-DR on exports, we are able to show how trade trends would have changed without the existence of the agreement. Figures C.1 and C.2 show CAFTA's estimated effect on bilateral trade flows (exports and imports, respectively) between Costa Rica and the United States. As the dotted line in figure C.1 indicates, exports to the

United States are estimated to have been greater than they would have had there not been a free trade agreement. This result is highly significant although in terms of magnitude it is relatively small as each quarter the effect of CAFTA-DR is estimated to have increased export growth by 5.6 percent.[5] Similarly for imports, as the dotted line in figure C.2 indicates, imports from the United States are estimated to have been greater than they would have had there not been a free trade agreement. However, this effect was not significant.

Table C.1 OLS Estimation of Equation (1) Exports

Variables	(a) X_t^{ij}	(b) X_t^{ij}	(c) X_t^{ij}
X_{t-1}^{ij}	−0.491***	−0.491***	−0.446***
	(0.113)	(0.114)	(0.119)
GDP_{t-1}^i	−0.677	−0.676	−0.240
	(0.760)	(0.775)	(0.800)
GDP_{t-2}^i	1.320*	1.321*	1.516*
	(0.720)	(0.737)	(0.775)
GDP_{t-3}^i	0.978	0.979	1.248
	(0.724)	(0.748)	(0.783)
GDP_{t-4}^i	−1.816***	−1.815***	−1.840***
	(0.630)	(0.641)	(0.678)
GDP_{t-4}^j	2.371*	2.370*	1.152
	(1.363)	(1.388)	(1.379)
P_{t-1}^i	−1.122***	−1.122***	−1.100**
	(0.405)	(0.415)	(0.439)
P_{t-1}^j	1.810	1.820	5.966
	(3.218)	(3.832)	(3.675)
E_{t-1}^{ij}	−0.335	−0.336	−0.0884
	(0.514)	(0.536)	(0.558)
E_{t-1}^{jw}	0.261**	0.261**	0.265**
	(0.103)	(0.106)	(0.112)
CAFTA$_{04}$	0.0543***	n.a.	n.a.
	(0.0177)	n.a.	n.a.
CAFTA$_{04-09}$	n.a.	0.0542**	n.a.
	n.a.	(0.0211)	n.a.
CAFTA$_{09}$	n.a.	0.0544**	0.0351
	n.a.	(0.0228)	(0.0228)
Constant	−0.0193	−0.0193	−0.0225
	(0.0218)	(0.0270)	(0.0286)
Observations	59	59	59
R-squared	0.489	0.489	0.416

Note: Standard errors in parentheses; n.a. = not applicable; OLS = ordinary least squares.
*** $p < 0.01$, ** $p < 0.05$, * $p < 0.1$.

Table C.2 OLS Estimation of Equation (2) Imports

Variables	(a) M_t^{ij}	(b) M_t^{ij}	(c) M_t^{ij}
M_{t-1}^{ij}	−0.154	−0.162	−0.162
	(0.122)	(0.122)	(0.120)
M_{t-2}^{ij}	−0.100	−0.111	−0.111
	(0.120)	(0.120)	(0.118)
M_{t-3}^{ij}	−0.0341	−0.0524	−0.0524
	(0.117)	(0.118)	(0.116)
M_{t-4}^{ij}	−0.600***	−0.595***	−0.595***
	(0.117)	(0.117)	(0.115)
GDP_{t-1}^{i}	2.863**	3.021**	3.021**
	(1.217)	(1.229)	(1.191)
GDP_{t-2}^{i}	2.702**	2.396*	2.397**
	(1.176)	(1.219)	(1.158)
GDP_{t-1}^{j}	3.288*	3.264*	3.264*
	(1.813)	(1.815)	(1.789)
GDP_{t-2}^{j}	0.352	0.407	0.406
	(1.768)	(1.771)	(1.620)
GDP_{t-3}^{j}	−5.520***	−5.604***	−5.605***
	(1.689)	(1.693)	(1.604)
P_{t-1}^{i}	1.835***	1.697**	1.698***
	(0.609)	(0.626)	(0.599)
P_{t-2}^{i}	1.359**	1.163*	1.164*
	(0.651)	(0.683)	(0.654)
P_{t-1}^{j}	−6.641	−8.962	−8.958*
	(5.024)	(5.576)	(5.040)
E_{t-1}^{ij}	−0.393	−0.211	−0.211
	(0.829)	(0.851)	(0.825)
E_{t-2}^{ij}	1.559**	1.679**	1.679**
	(0.754)	(0.765)	(0.755)
E_{t-3}^{ij}	1.165	1.016	1.017
	(0.729)	(0.746)	(0.730)
E_{t-4}^{ij}	1.089	1.187	1.187*
	(0.707)	(0.715)	(0.690)
E_{t-1}^{iw}	0.176	0.155	0.155
	(0.112)	(0.114)	(0.112)
E_{t-2}^{iw}	−0.303**	−0.318***	−0.318***
	(0.116)	(0.117)	(0.113)
E_{t-3}^{iw}	−0.275**	−0.284**	−0.284**
	(0.122)	(0.123)	(0.117)
E_{t-4}^{iw}	−0.548***	−0.532***	−0.532***
	(0.164)	(0.165)	(0.159)

table continues next page

Table C.2 OLS Estimation of Equation (2) Imports *(continued)*

	(a)	*(b)*	*(c)*
Variables	M_t^{ij}	M_t^{ij}	M_t^{ij}
CAFTA$_{04}$	−0.0109	n.a.	n.a.
	(0.0263)	n.a.	n.a.
CAFTA$_{04-09}$	n.a.	5.84e−05	n.a.
	n.a.	(0.0287)	n.a.
CAFTA$_{09}$	n.a.	−0.0300	−0.0300
	n.a.	(0.0330)	(0.0282)
Constant	−0.0424	−0.0202	−0.0202
	(0.0297)	(0.0376)	(0.0368)
Observations	59	59	59
R-squared	0.679	0.687	0.687

Note: Standard errors in parentheses; n.a. = not applicable; OLS = ordinary least squares.
*** $p < 0.01$, ** $p < 0.05$, * $p < 0.1$.

Figure C.1 Costa Rican Quarterly Exports to the United States, 1997–2012

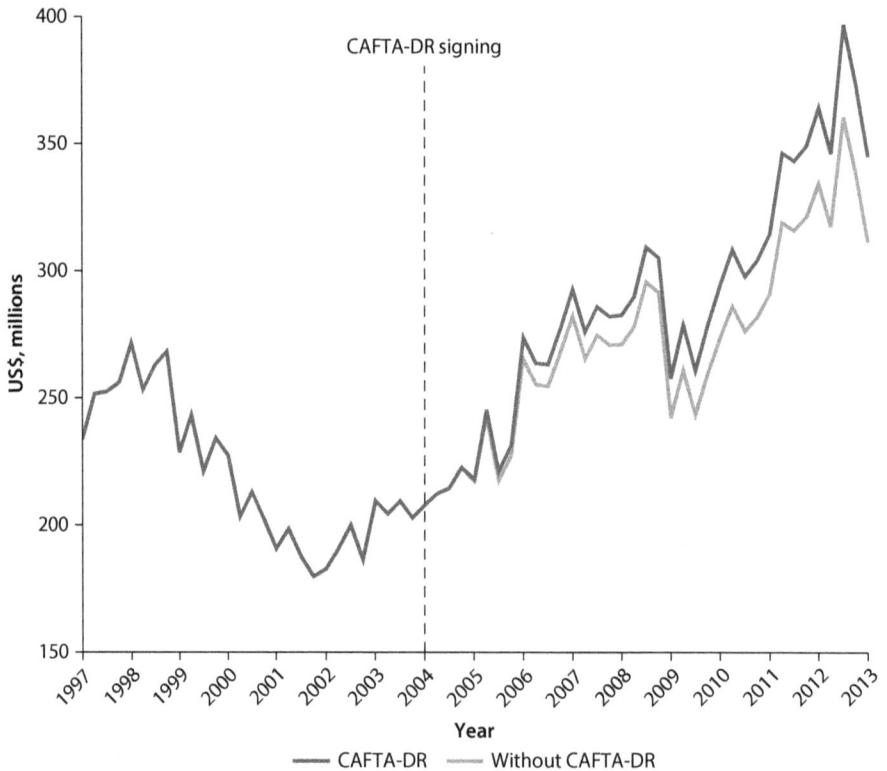

Sources: Estimations based on data from the Central Bank of Costa Rica (BCCR), Bureau of Economic Analysis, and National Institute of Statistics and Census (*Instituto Nacional de Estadísticas y Censos* [INEC]).

Figure C.2 Costa Rican Quarterly Imports from the United States, 1997–2012

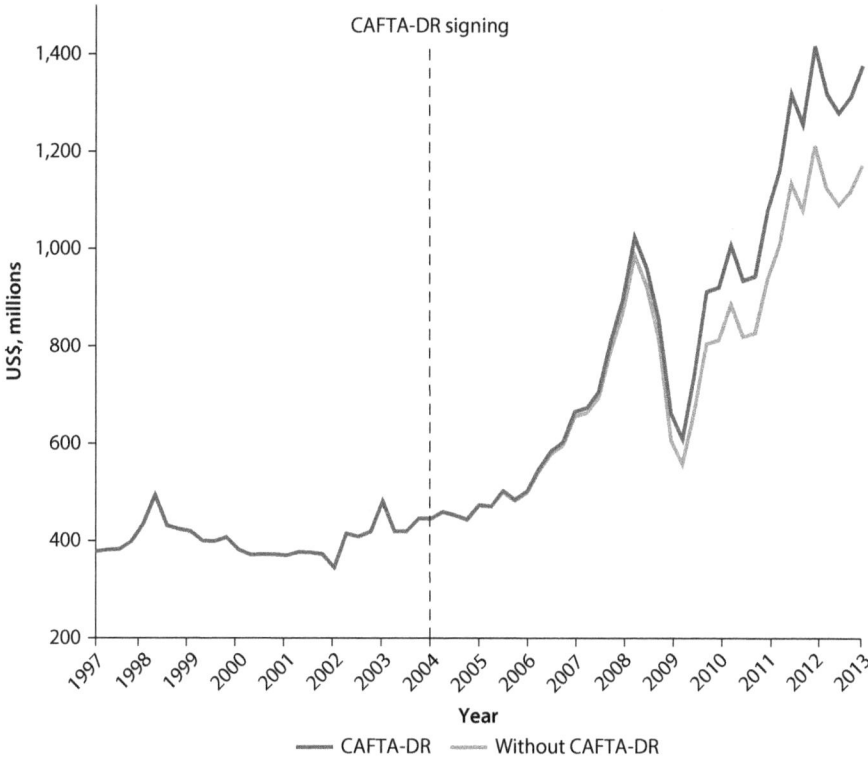

Sources: Estimations based on data from the Central Bank of Costa Rica (BCCR), Bureau of Economic Analysis, and National Institute of Statistics and Census (*Instituto Nacional de Estadísticas y Censos* [INEC]).
Note: The data exclude exports from the free trade zones.

Notes

1. The real effective exchange rate between the United States and the rest of the world was calculated using Costa Rica's 13 main trading partners and using their respective consumer price indices.
2. The methodology used to determine these lags and select the model is discussed in the Methodology section.
3. The methodology used to determine these lags and select the model is discussed in the Methodology section.
4. Although CAFTA-DR was not ratified until five years later in January 1, 2009, the effects on trade were evidenced since its signing in 2004.
5. For the semi-logarithmic functional form presented in model (1), the coefficient associated with the CAFTA dummy cannot be interpreted as the percentage impact on the log first difference of X of a change in the dummy variable CAFTA from 0 to 1 status. The correct expression for this percentage change impact is $e^{\alpha_9} - 1$.

References

Anderson, J. 1979. "A Theoretical Foundation for the Gravity Equation." *American Economic Review* 69 (1): 106–16.

Bergstrand, J. 1985. "The Gravity Equation in International Trade: Some Microeconomic Foundations and Empirical Evidence." *The Review of Economics and Statistics* 67 (3): 474–81.

Gould, D. 1998. "Has NAFTA Changed North American Trade?" *Federal Reserve Bank of Dallas Economic Review* First Quarter: 12–23.

Jaramillo, F., and D. Lederman. 2006. *Challenges of CAFTA: Maximizing the Benefits for Central America*. Directions in Development Trade. Washington, DC: World Bank.

Environmental Benefits Statement

The World Bank Group is committed to reducing its environmental footprint. In support of this commitment, the Publishing and Knowledge Division leverages electronic publishing options and print-on-demand technology, which is located in regional hubs worldwide. Together, these initiatives enable print runs to be lowered and shipping distances decreased, resulting in reduced paper consumption, chemical use, greenhouse gas emissions, and waste.

The Publishing and Knowledge Division follows the recommended standards for paper use set by the Green Press Initiative. Whenever possible, books are printed on 50 percent to 100 percent postconsumer recycled paper, and at least 50 percent of the fiber in our book paper is either unbleached or bleached using Totally Chlorine Free (TCF), Processed Chlorine Free (PCF), or Enhanced Elemental Chlorine Free (EECF) processes.

More information about the Bank's environmental philosophy can be found at http://crinfo.worldbank.org/wbcrinfo/node/4.

green
press
INITIATIVE

www.ingramcontent.com/pod-product-compliance
Lightning Source LLC
Chambersburg PA
CBHW080559220326
41599CB00032B/6534